THE THREE PILLAR MODEL
FOR BUSINESS DECISIONS:
Strategy, Law and Ethics

George Siedel
University of Michigan

Published by Van Rye Publishing, LLC
www.vanryepublishing.com

ISBN-10: 0-9970566-0-6
ISBN-13: 978-0-9970566-0-0

About the Author

George Siedel is the Williamson Family Professor of Business Administration and the Thurnau Professor of Business Law at the University of Michigan. He teaches courses on business law, negotiation, and public policy at Michigan's Ross School of Business and in seminars worldwide to business leaders, consultants, entrepreneurs, attorneys, and other professionals.

Professor Siedel completed his graduate studies at the University of Michigan and Cambridge University. He has served as a visiting professor at Stanford University and Harvard University and as a Visiting Scholar at University of California, Berkeley. As a Fulbright Scholar, he held a Distinguished Chair in the Humanities and Social Sciences.

Professor Siedel has received several national research awards including the Maurer Award, the Ralph Bunche Award, and the Hoeber Award. He is the author of the best-selling book *Negotiating for Success: Essential Strategies and Skills*. He has also received numerous teaching awards, including the recent Executive Program Professor of the Year Award from CIMBA, an international consortium of thirty-six leading universities.

Hundreds of thousands of learners have taken Professor Siedel's Massive Open Online Course ("MOOC") on "Successful Negotiation: Essential Strategies and Skills" (which is offered by the University of Michigan and Coursera), making it one of the most popular MOOCs of all time. In conjunction with the course, Professor Siedel developed a free app for negotiation planning, which is available at http://www.negotiationplanner.com.

Acknowledgments

Although I am listed as the author, this book is the product of the shared advice, experience, and wisdom of thousands of business leaders, entrepreneurs, consultants, attorneys, colleagues, students, and others. I am unable to mention them all, but listed below is a sampling (in alphabetical order by surname or organization name).

I also acknowledge the outstanding researchers whose work has improved business decision-making theory and practice over the years. This book includes citations to many of their publications. In an era of powerful search engines, detailed citations are unnecessary. Instead, brief citations like the ones in this book provide enough information to enable you to easily locate the sources.

The book also includes many citations to primary legal sources. However, discussions of the law in this book are not intended and should not be construed as legal advice.

In addition to the acknowledgments that follow, I acknowledge and thank the publishers of my earlier books that relate to the Three Pillar model. Chapters 2 and 3 have been adapted and updated from my book *Using the Law for Competitive Advantage* (Jossey-Bass) and Chapters 6 and 7 are adapted from my book *Negotiating for Success: Essential Strategies and Skills* (Van Rye Publishing, LLC).

Business Leaders, Entrepreneurs, and Professionals. Thank you to the business leaders, entrepreneurs, and professionals from Africa, Asia, Australia, Europe, North America, and South America with whom I have worked over the years. In addition to teaching open seminars for business leaders, I have offered seminars and given presentations to specific audiences that include athletic directors, attorneys, consultants, entrepreneurs, physicians, and senior executives. Whether teaching in Mumbai, Sao Paulo, Seoul, Sydney, or Venice, I have learned from these participants that the decision-making concepts covered in this book are valuable in all professions, in all cultures, and on all continents.

David E. A. Carson. Thank you to David, a successful business leader, prominent alumnus of the Ross School of Business and friend, for establishing the Carson Scholars Program ("CSP"). CSP is a pioneering program that provides public policy education to business school students. Through my position as CSP Director, I have had the opportunity to work with distinguished governmental leaders in Washington who have shared their insights into behind-the-scenes strategies and tactics that are discussed in Chapter 4.

Center for Positive Organizations. My thanks to my friends and colleagues at the Center for Positive Organizations ("CPO"), where I am a Faculty Associate, for encouraging the research that led to the publication of this book. CPO is the world's leading center for research on Positive Organizational Scholarship. The Center's mission, which is aligned perfectly with the Three Pillar model for decision making, "is to inspire and enable leaders to build high-performing organizations that bring out the best in people."

Harvard Business School. Thank you to Harvard Business School ("HBS") for providing a welcoming and supportive academic environment when I was a Visiting Professor of Business Administration. It was when serving on a teaching committee at HBS that I first realized the practical benefits from using the three foundations for business decision making: economics, law, and ethics. The Three Pillar model in this book builds on these foundations.

Helena Haapio. Many thanks to my frequent coauthor Helena Haapio, International Contract Counsel for Lexpert Ltd. in Helsinki, Finland, and a leader in the Proactive Law Movement. Helena has been an inspiration in her ability to integrate the theoretical and practical aspects of law. Parts of Chapter 6 are adapted from our book *A Short Guide to Contract Risk* (Gower 2013) and from our 2010 article, "Using Proactive Law for Competitive Advantage" in the *American Business Law Journal*. I am also grateful to Helena for introducing me to the visualization community. Contract visualization is discussed in Chapter 6.

Nancy Hauptman. Thank you to Nancy for her thorough review of the manuscript, for her creative design work on the figures that appear throughout the book, and for her support and encouragement in general.

Christine Ladwig. A special thank you to Christine, a professor at the Harrison College of Business at Southeast Missouri State University, who wrote Chapter 5 on intellectual property. Christine is highly educated in law and science with five graduate degrees, including a Ph.D. in biology and an LL.M. in Intellectual Property. The Academy of Legal Studies in Business selected Christine as a finalist for the prestigious Charles M. Hewitt Master Teacher Award in honor of her teaching in the field of intellectual property.

MOOC Students. Thank you to the hundreds of thousands of students worldwide who have taken my Massive Open Online Course, "Successful Negotiation: Essential Strategies and Skills," which is offered by the University of Michigan in partnership with Coursera. Their positive feedback and success stories reinforce the Chapter 6 discussion of value-creating contracts.

Lynn Sharp Paine. A special thank you to Professor Lynn Sharp Paine, McLean Professor of Business Administration and Senior Associate Dean at Harvard Business School, whose work is highlighted in Chapter 8. Through her leadership position and her business ethics teaching and research, Lynn is a role model for anyone interested in the Ethics Pillar of decision-making.

Ross School Students. A special thank you to the undergraduate and MBA students who have taken my courses at the Ross School of Business. One of my joys in teaching is the continuing opportunity to learn from this diverse body of students from around the world. Through their talent, enthusiasm, and desire to develop businesses that serve both the interests of shareholders and society, these students inspire confidence about the future role of business.

John Siedel. This book would not have been possible without John's outstanding technical ability and editorial skills throughout the writing and publication process.

Leslie Southwick Wilhelm. Last, but certainly not least, my thank you to Leslie Southwick Wilhelm of Writing Works, LLC for her outstanding editorial work. I especially appreciate her kind manner when making suggestions for improvement. Any grammatical errors in the book are the result of my failure to heed Leslie's excellent advice.

George Siedel
University of Michigan

Contents

Introduction

This is a book about competition. We live in a global economy that is driven by fierce competition for business and career success. If you are not interested in participating in this competition, please read no further.

For those of you with drive and a competitive spirit, my goal in writing this book is to help you succeed. This requires that you understand the three pillars that are the foundation of business decisions: strategy, law, and ethics. Understanding these pillars is also valuable when you make any type of personal or leadership decision.

I first became acquainted with three pillar thinking in 1997 when my friend Tim Fort, who holds the Everleigh Chair at Indiana University, published a seminal article on three forces that shape decision-making—economics, law, and ethics. The following year, when I served as a Visiting Professor of Business Administration at Harvard Business School ("HBS"), I discovered that every Harvard MBA student was required to take a module that introduced them to those same three forces. HBS eventually expanded the module into a required course on leadership.

In this book, I have revised the three forces from Fort's research and from the Harvard course by replacing "economics" with "strategy." Strategy is based in part on economics, but provides a broader perspective that can be used in all types of business, leadership, and personal decisions. With this change, I began to use the Three Pillar nomenclature.

This book takes you through four steps that enable you to use the Three Pillar model for business decisions:

Step One: Become a legally savvy leader. This does not require memorization of legal rules. Instead, you should understand how the law works in practice. Various surveys have identified the key legal areas that every business leader should understand: product liability, employment law, government regulation, intellectual property, contracts, and dispute resolution.

This book provides briefings on each area and shows how they impact your key stakeholders: customers, employees, government, and investors.

Step Two: Become an effective risk manager. After your briefings on the law, you are now ready to focus on the Law Pillar. The Law Pillar emphasizes risk management. This book explains how to manage the legal risks that constitute the main threat to your business success. For example, the chapter on product liability will describe how to make strategic new product decisions, how to isolate product risks by creating subsidiaries, and how to design new products to minimize the risk of being sued for selling a defective product.

Step Three: Align the Strategy Pillar with the Law Pillar to create value. Many leaders think that there is an inherent tension between the Strategy Pillar, with its value creation orientation, and the Law Pillar, with its risk management orientation. This book explains how you can overcome this tension and align the two pillars by focusing on the interests of each of your stakeholders. For example, by focusing on customer interests, a process designed to prevent product liability can be transformed into a powerful product development tool.

Step Four: Develop an ethical organization. Understanding the Ethics Pillar of decision making enables you to play a leadership role in developing compliance and values standards for your organization. This role requires that you "walk the talk" by using a principled process for making ethical decisions. By combining the Ethics Pillar with the Law Pillar and the Strategy Pillar, you can become a responsible corporate citizen while at the same time creating value for your shareholders and other stakeholders.

According to a quote attributed to J. Irwin Miller, former CEO of Cummins, Inc., "A healthy branch cannot survive on a rotten trunk." I hope that this book will enable you to grow a healthy branch—your business—while also nourishing the healthy trunk that symbolizes the environment in which business operates.

I INTRODUCTION TO THE THREE PILLAR MODEL

1   The Three Pillar Model for Business Decisions

While your friend is driving to your apartment, you develop a sudden craving for pizza and place an order with a nearby restaurant. You then text your friend and ask her to pick up the pizza on the way to your apartment.

President Barack Obama decides, in his words, "to make the killing or capture of Osama bin Laden the top priority of our war against al Qaeda." He then authorizes the operation that results in bin Laden's death.

What does your personal decision to buy a pizza have in common with the President's leadership decision?

Both scenarios illustrate the Three Pillars that provide the foundation for decisions in business, leadership, and everyday life: strategy, law, and ethics. This book focuses on the Three Pillars as they relate to business decisions. But these pillars are also important when making a variety of decisions beyond business, ranging from your personal decision to order a pizza to the President's decision to authorize the bin Laden operation.

Let's start with the pizza example. You probably did not complete a Three Pillar analysis when deciding to ask your friend to pick up your dinner. But had you done so, your focus would have been only on the Strategy Pillar. In the language of strategy, your decision focused on "formulating" and "implementing" a strategy.

You formulated your strategic goal—acquiring a pizza—and developed an implementation plan that involved ordering the pizza and texting your friend to ask her to pick it up. In all likelihood, you did not consider the legal and ethical implications of your strategy. But your failure to consider the Law and Ethics Pillars does not mean they were absent. And this failure might have dramatic consequences for you, your friend, and others.

Consider the case of *Kubert v. Best*, decided in 2013 by an appellate court in New Jersey. The case resulted from an accident on September 21, 2009. A husband and wife were riding a motorcycle when a pickup truck heading in the opposite direction crossed the center line and struck them. The husband and wife were severely injured and their left legs had to be amputated. Immediately before the accident, a friend sent a text message to the truck driver, and he responded by texting a reply. The husband and wife sued both the driver and his friend. They settled with the driver, and the case proceeded against the friend who sent the message.

The court noted that under New Jersey law, it is illegal to drive while using a cell phone that is not hands-free, and a driver who injures someone using a hand-held cell phone is subject to a possible prison sentence. But this case's resolution did not turn on criminal law or the driver's involvement. Instead, the issue was whether someone who sends a text to a driver can be held liable for damages. The court decided that "the sender of a text message can potentially be liable if an accident is caused by texting… if the sender knew or had special reason to know that the recipient would view the text while driving and thus be distracted." Despite this potential liability, the court decided that the friend who sent the text was not liable in this case because there was no proof that she "knew or had special reason to know that the driver would read the message while driving…."

As this case illustrates, when you are considering the strategic decision (the Strategy Pillar) of whether and how to obtain a pizza, you should also consider whether your decision is legal (the Law Pillar). In this situation, the Law Pillar of decision making requires you to consider liability for damages. This pillar also involves decision making under uncertainty. For example, if you aren't in New Jersey, how likely is it that the country or state where you are located will apply a rule similar to the New Jersey rule? And even if you are in New Jersey, do the facts in your case fall within the rule? In other words, how likely is it that a jury would decide that you knew or had a special reason to know that your friend would read the text while driving?

If you are risk averse, you probably would decide to change your strategy implementation plan by, say, asking the restaurant to deliver the pizza or making the pizza yourself. But even if you proceed as originally planned despite the legal risk, you must still consider the Ethics Pillar. Is it ethical to place your friend (and others) at risk by texting her while she is driving? Considering the Ethics Pillar is important even when you are absolutely certain that your decisions are legal.

Let's now move from this personal decision to leadership decision making—President Obama's decision to authorize the operation that led to bin Laden's death. The President and his advisors initially focused on the Strategy Pillar as they formulated the strategy to capture or kill bin Laden. They also developed an implementation plan—the raid on bin Laden's compound.

With a strategy in place, the President then focused on the Law Pillar. His strategy, like virtually any other personal, business, or leadership strategy, raised several legal questions. Three questions were especially important: did the President have the legal right to "authorize a lethal mission, to delay telling Congress until afterward, and to bury a wartime enemy [bin Laden] at sea"?[1]

According to an account in *The New York Times*,[2] a few days before the raid a top-secret team of four lawyers provided the President with legal advice relating to these questions. As with most legal advice, the law was not entirely clear. And like other political or business leaders, the President had to decide whether to proceed under conditions of legal uncertainty. In addition, even if the law clearly supported the strategy, the President still had to consider the Ethics Pillar: What were the ethical ramifications of authorizing a mission to kill bin Laden?

As these examples illustrate, the Three Pillar model provides the framework for everyday decisions as simple as ordering a pizza and leadership decisions as complex as the bin Laden raid. This model is especially important in making business decisions, which are the focus of this book. Business decision makers who overemphasize the Strategy Pillar to the detriment of the Law and Ethics Pillars risk destroying their companies and careers.

Origins of the Three Pillar Model

The Three Pillar Model's Theoretical Foundations

The Three Pillar model has foundations in naturalistic, philosophical, and sociological theories. In "How Relationality Shapes Business Ethics," Timothy L. Fort (Everleigh Chair in Business Ethics in the Business Law and Ethics Department at Indiana University's Kelley School of Business) provides an insightful analysis of the Three Pillar model's origins. The end result of his analysis is a framework that enables business leaders to take "into account all the forces that are a natural part of human life" when making decisions. These forces are based on "legal, economic, and ecologizing (integrity-based) values."[3]

Emphasizing a corporate social responsibility perspective but arriving at a conclusion similar to Fort's model, Archie B. Carroll (a professor emeritus at the University of Georgia's Terry College of Business) and Mark S. Schwartz (a business law and ethics professor at York University) developed a three-domain model that builds on earlier work by Carroll. In their model, the three overlapping domains are economic, legal, and ethical.

Their concept of the economic domain covers activities designed to have a positive economic impact on a business, specifically "(i) the maximization of profits and/or (ii) the maximization of share value." They divide the legal domain into three categories: compliance, avoidance of civil litigation, and anticipation of changes in legislation. The ethical domain "refers to the ethical responsibilities of business as expected by the general population and relevant stakeholders."[4]

Translating Theory into Practice:
The Harvard Model

The clearest practical perspective on the Three Pillar model comes from the Harvard Business School ("HBS"). I first encountered this perspective in 1998 when I was a Visiting Professor of Business Administration at Harvard and served on the teaching committee for a module called "Leadership, Values and Decision Making" that was taught to all students entering the MBA program at HBS.

Although the module appeared to successfully address the intersection of economic, legal, and ethical issues that shape business decisions, faculty members at Harvard "examined the need to teach more about business law" in light of the globalization of business and increased use of technology.[5] The faculty eventually voted to expand the module into an entire course that all MBA students would be required to take. Following input from many stakeholders (students, alumni, advisory boards, etc.), the course was offered for the first time in 2004 under the name "Leadership and Corporate Accountability" ("LCA").

Professor Lynn Sharp Paine was one of the key leaders in developing the course. Paine, the John G. McLean Professor at Harvard Business School, holds a law degree from Harvard and a doctorate in moral philosophy from Oxford. Although she has earned international renown for high-quality research, Paine emphasizes the practical focus when she describes the course: "We are training future practitioners.... We focus not on rare events or abstract issues in moral philosophy, but on decisions that students will have to make in their careers."[6]

LCA focuses on three key elements—economics, law, and ethics—that form the foundation for decision-making in business. As described in the 2011 online version of the course syllabus, a business leader's responsibilities "fall into three broad categories: economic, legal, and ethical. Economic responsibilities relate to resource allocation and wealth creation; legal responsibilities flow from formal laws and regulations; and ethical responsibilities have to do with basic principles and standards of conduct."[7]

The HBS course mirrors the theoretical work by Fort, Carroll and Schwartz: "Using the tripartite framework of economics, law, and ethics, we will consider decisions that involve responsibilities to each of the company's core constituencies—investors, customers, employees, suppliers, and the public." Outside the Harvard course, these constituencies are often called stakeholders—i.e., those who have an interest (a "stake") in the business.

Like other courses at HBS, LCA is not static and continues to evolve to reflect new issues and cases. The 2011 online syllabus illustrates the types of issues addressed in the course that relate to the four constituencies. These issues include fiduciary duties, insider trading, conflicts of interest, product liability, fraud, the employment-at-will doctrine, labor law, discrimination, environmental responsibility, privacy, and property rights.

The course is especially challenging and important because it takes students beyond the basics covered in introductory courses on finance, marketing, operations, and so on into what the syllabus calls the "grey areas" of business. These real-world grey areas are shaped by the analytical perspectives of the economics, law, and ethics triad that are a staple of everyday business decision-making. The overlap of the three perspectives is depicted by a diagram from a course overview that students receive at the beginning of LCA.

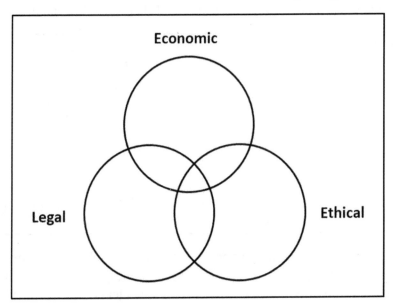

As the course overview notes, "The basic idea is that outstanding managers develop plans of action that fall in the 'sweet spot' at the intersection of their economic, legal, and ethical responsibilities."[8] The course guide for instructors elaborates on what is also described as the "zone of sustainability":[9]

> Actions and strategies that fall inside this zone tend to be acceptable to the firm's constituencies and thus repeatable over time, while those that lie outside typically invite negative repercussions from injured, wronged, or otherwise disappointed parties. Actions outside the zone may even lead to the firm's failure, especially if pursued at length.

The three dimensions of the Harvard model can also be depicted in the form of a decision tree adapted from a diagram developed by

9

Constance Bagley, a senior research scholar at Yale who previously held business law appointments at the HBS and the Stanford Graduate School of Business. Originally appearing in "The Ethical Leader's Decision Tree,"[10] the tree is reproduced in a recent article Bagley coauthored with Mark Roellig and Gianmarco Massameno.[11]

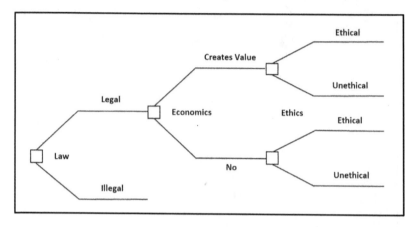

The ideal decision making path would follow the Legal, Creates Value, and Ethical branches, although in some cases another path might be justified. For example, business leaders might decide to take an action that benefits society even if it doesn't create economic value for shareholders. But this decision would raise legal concerns that will be addressed later in this chapter.

Expanding the Harvard Model

The Harvard model and the decision tree provide a valuable framework for making business decisions. However, by expanding the economics perspective the model also becomes useful in making decisions beyond the business sphere.

While economics is a key discipline relating to the business goal of value creation, other disciplines and functions also contribute to business success. Business school courses are based on three disciplines in addition to economics—law, psychology, and statistics. The landmark Carnegie study of business education, for instance, recommended that business schools place "heavy weight on preparation in the four foundation areas—quantitative methods, economics, law and public policy, and psychology-sociology," with two required three-credit courses on regulation and law.[12]

Business success depends on key functions that draw on these disciplines. As noted in the opening sentence of a *Harvard Business Review* article on business functions: "Business units come and go, but finance, HR, IT, marketing, legal, and R&D are forever."[13]

The departmental organization of business schools often mirrors key business functions. For example, at the University of Michigan's Ross School of Business the economics discipline is represented by a Business Economics area, while other academic areas reflect the seven key business functions that are present in virtually every major company: (1) Accounting, (2) Business Law, (3) Finance, (4) Management & Organizations, (5) Marketing, (6) Strategy, and (7) Technology & Operations.

Departments at the University of Pennsylvania's Wharton School are organized along the same lines, except that Strategy is included in the Management Department and there are three additional departments—two industry-related (Health Care Management and Real Estate) and one discipline-related (Statistics).

The "Big Seven" functions represented in both company and business school organizational structures are critical to the success of businesses of all sizes. The most important issues facing an entrepreneur starting a business, for example, relate to accounting, financing, legal, marketing, operations, staffing, and strategic concerns.

Strategy is the most likely candidate among the seven functions as a replacement for economics. Defined broadly, strategy involves establishing and achieving goals. In a business setting, strategy focuses on the goal of value creation for shareholders, which brings into play all functions and disciplines, including economics.

Strategy is also an attractive candidate because it is important in all organizations, even non-profits that are not concerned with creating shareholder value. And on a personal level, your strategic ability to establish and achieve goals is also key to your success, however you choose to define it. So by replacing economics with strategy, the Three Pillar model becomes a framework that is more appropriate for all forms of business, leadership, and personal decision making.

The Three Pillar Model for Business Decisions

Although the Three Pillar model can be applied within all organizations (public or private, business or non-profit) and when making personal decisions as simple as ordering a pizza, this book focuses on using the model to make business decisions. The key questions that business decision makers should address are:

1. Strategy Pillar: What is our value creation goal and how do we intend to achieve it? (*Note: After a strategic plan has been formulated, the remaining two pillars can be considered in either order.*)

2. Law Pillar: How can we manage the legal risks associated with our strategy?

3. Ethics Pillar: Is our proposed strategic decision ethical?

We now examine each of the pillars as they relate to business before turning to the major challenge in using the Three Pillar model—the gap between the Strategy Pillar and the Law Pillar.

The Strategy Pillar

According to Pulitzer Prize-winning historian Alfred Chandler, "Strategy is the determination of the basic long-term goals of an enterprise, and the adoption of courses of action and the allocation of resources necessary for carrying out these goals."[14] This definition states the twin aspects of business strategy (as well as other types of strategy): formulating goals and planning for implementation. The late Yogi Berra, a baseball legend, summarized the risk in not having a strategic plan: "If you don't know where you are going, you might wind up someplace else."

The goal in business is often framed in terms of value creation. Harvard professor Michael Porter summarizes the two key issues that form the basis of strategic choice as (1) the attractiveness of industries and (2) the competitive position within an industry.

Industry attractiveness, according to Porter, is determined by "five competitive forces: the entry of new competitors, the threat of substitutes, the bargaining power of buyers, the bargaining power of suppliers, and the rivalry among the existing competitors." Competitive position within an industry is based on value creation and "superior value stems from offering lower prices than competitors for equivalent benefits or providing unique benefits that more than offset a higher price."[15]

Business leaders often frame their goals in terms of value creation for shareholders. The so-called "shareholder primacy" theory asserts that shareholders should have top priority over other corporate stakeholders. This theory has been criticized because, in emphasizing shareholder profits, it allegedly encourages short-term thinking. The legal foundations of this theory are analyzed later in this chapter.

The Law Pillar

According to *Black's Law Dictionary*, law represents "A system of principles and rules of human conduct...." In a business setting, law represents the "rules of the game," the framework for business operations and decision making. As a manager in one of my executive courses put it, law provides the architecture in which business is conducted.

Whereas law has always been a key element in business success, its importance accelerated in the last half of the 20th century. Chayes, Greenwald, and Wing in a *Harvard Business Review* article published in 1983[16] referred to the "growth in the scope, nature, and complexity of government regulation" and the "equally rapid rise in consumer, shareholder, employee, and competitor litigation" in concluding that managers need "to include legal advice as an essential element of business planning and decision making."

More recently, the global dimension of business has enhanced the role of law in business decision making. The first question an investor should raise when considering an investment in another country is this: "Does this country have a rule of law or, instead, will the company be subject to the arbitrary whims of government officials?"

This question became especially important after market systems developed in former Communist countries. As George Melloan observed, writing in the *Wall Street Journal*, a market system cannot be established in an emerging economy "without first creating a legal system that protects the right of all individuals to hold, buy or sell property and without corresponding legal protections for the contracts through which those transactions are conducted."[17]

Once you decide that your target country follows the rule of law, you must then understand what the law requires. As Carolyn

Hotchkiss (who teaches business law and serves as Dean at Babson College) has observed:

> Law provides the ground rules for international trade and investment in goods, services and technology. An understanding of the ground rules for that trade and investment allows managers to compete successfully in the most competitive global markets. A working understanding of the international legal environment allows managers to make judgments about the political and business risk of doing business in countries around the world.[18]

Echoing this observation, Jere Morehead, President of the University of Georgia (who is the Meigs Professor of Legal Studies in the Terry College of Business), has emphasized the importance of international business law courses in business schools.[19] And a survey of business leaders presented at the 2014 conference on the Internationalization of US Education in the 21st Century concluded that the two most important international skills that companies seek in their professional staff and line managers are an appreciation for cross-cultural differences and an understanding of legal/government requirements.[20]

Surveys of senior executives highlight the importance of the Law Pillar. For example, sessions on law ranked third (behind only Organization Behavior and Finance) in terms of value provided to participants, according to executive program evaluations completed by more than 900 senior managers attending general, industry, and functional executive programs at the University of Michigan.[21]

This high ranking of law is not surprising given the considerable amount of time business leaders spend on legal issues. Although studies over the years have concluded that leaders spend a high percentage of their time on legal matters, prominent management scholar Henry Mintzberg published the most telling research in his

Harvard Business Review classic "The Manager's Job: Folklore and Fact."[22] In this article, Mintzberg describes the four roles that managers play as decision makers: entrepreneur, resource allocator, disturbance handler, and negotiator.

He concludes that managers act as *entrepreneurs* when trying to improve the business and adapt it to a changing environment. They act as *resource allocators* in making budgeting decisions, authorizing projects, and designing the organizational structure. Both of these roles are replete with legal issues relating to new product development, marketing plans, department reorganization, mergers and acquisitions, and so on.

Law becomes even more important when managers play their other two roles. Mintzberg notes that as *disturbance handlers*, managers must respond involuntarily when "pressures of a situation are too severe to be ignored—a strike looms, a major customer has gone bankrupt, or a supplier reneges on a contract...."

The manager's role as a *negotiator* is equally important. In Mintzberg's words, "Managers spend considerable time in negotiations: the president of the football team works out a contract with the holdout superstar; the corporation president leads the company's contingent to negotiate a new strike issue; the foreman argues a grievance problem to its conclusion with the shop steward." These negotiations are filled with legal issues because, to cite a familiar adage, negotiation takes place within the shadow of the law.

In addition to these four roles that require them to become legal decision makers, managers are legal communicators. They must be prepared to discuss legal matters with all company stakeholders—notably investors (and their representatives, the Board of Directors), creditors, customers, employees, suppliers, and government regulators.

Managers' decisional and communication roles increase as they move up the ranks. It is no surprise that they spend considerable time with their lawyers. As the CEO of United States Steel Corporation recently put it, "The CEO and the GC [General Counsel] must have the kind of relationship in which they're able to practically finish each other's sentences."[23]

The Law Pillar's importance extends beyond its impact on managers in large companies. For example, entrepreneurs starting a business must make decisions regarding

- the legal form of their business,
- government regulations that govern how they develop and market their products and services,
- liability risks in manufacturing and selling their products,
- protecting their intellectual property,
- the nature of their contracts with customers and suppliers,
- legal considerations relating to financing the business, and
- the law that governs hiring employees.

It is no surprise that legendary entrepreneur David Packard, co-founder of Hewlett-Packard, concluded that business law and management accounting were the most valuable courses he took at Stanford's Graduate School of Business.[24]

The Ethics Pillar

In broad terms, ethics focuses on determining whether conduct is right or wrong. According to the *Stanford Encyclopedia of Philosophy*, when applied to business, ethics is a discipline that focuses on the "moral features of commercial activity."

The Ethics Pillar is especially important because unethical conduct by one company can harm a broad swath of stakeholders, as illustrated by the emissions scandal involving Volkswagen ("VW") that erupted in late 2015. At the time, VW was the world's leader in car sales. Shortly after United States government regulators announced that VW had cheated on air pollution tests, VW CEO Martin Winterkorn stated that he was "deeply sorry that we have broken the trust of our customers and the public." The head of VW in the United States put it more bluntly: "Our company was dishonest [with the regulators].... We have totally screwed up."[25]

In addition to its obvious impact on the company, the scandal had a ripple effect on many stakeholders. The following Reuters headlines, in chronological order in the month following Winterkorn's announcement on September 20, 2015, reveal the impact not only on VW's leaders and shareholders, but also on Germany, the local community, government regulators, employees, the diesel industry, suppliers, and customers.

- Shareholders: "VW Shares Plunge on Emissions Scandal" (September 21, 2015)
- Germany: "Volkswagen Scandal Threatens 'Made in Germany' Image" (September 22, 2015)
- Community: "Diesel Scandal Casts Gloom Over VW's Home Town" (September 25, 2015)
- Regulators: "VW Scandal Exposes Cozy Ties Between Industry and Berlin" (September 26, 2015)
- Company Leaders: "Former VW Boss Investigated for Fraud" (September 28, 2015)
- Employees: "VW Halts Hiring at Financing Arm After Emissions Scandal" (September 30, 2015)
- Industry: "VW Rivals Risk Bigger Blow as Emissions Scandal Hits Diesel" (October 2, 2015)
- Suppliers: "Car Parts Maker... Says VW Suppliers Should Not Pay for Scandal" (October 8, 2015)
- Customers: "Volkswagen Diesel Owners in US Face Lost Value and Limbo" (October 19, 2015)

Not mentioned in these headlines is the potential health hazard to the public resulting from the company's violation of environmental regulations. In early 2016, Reuters reported that the United States government started a lawsuit against VW alleging violation of the Clean Air Act. VW faces potential fines of over $90 billion, which does not include fines from non-US regulators or damages from lawsuits filed by customers.

An editorial in the *Financial Times*[26] entitled "Bankers Not Only Ones Pushing Ethical Boundaries" discussed problems in the banking industry in recent years, such as the 2015 guilty pleas and settlements by banks charged with rigging foreign exchange and LIBOR rates. (These cases involved Barclays, Citicorp, Deutsche Bank, JP Morgan Chase, the Royal Bank of Scotland, and other banks that paid billions of dollars in fines and settlements.) The editorial then observed that in other industries "companies around the world are pushing ethical boundaries," citing a $2 billion accounting scandal at Toshiba and General Motors' $900 million settlement with United States regulators for covering up its faulty ignition switches that resulted in more than 100 deaths.

The examples in the editorial dramatically illustrate the consequences of improper conduct, but the headline referring to "pushing ethical boundaries" illustrates a popular misconception that the problems repose entirely within the realm of the Ethics Pillar. All of the cases mentioned in the editorial, like the VW scandal, involved violations of the law and illustrate the need for business leaders to understand both the Law Pillar and the Ethics Pillar. Writing in *The New York Times*, Robert Prentice (Ed & Molly Smith Professor of Business Law at the McCombs School of Business, University of Texas) observed that scandals such as Enron, WorldCom, and ImClone involved serious ethical lapses, but they also occurred "because their participants had an insufficient knowledge of, appreciation for and, yes, fear of the law."[27]

The fear of the law that Prentice mentions is justified, considering legal penalties that have both civil and criminal dimensions. Claims against BP for the Deepwater Horizon oil spill illustrate both types of consequences. In mid-2015, BP agreed to settle government claims for $18.7 billion. This settlement does not include an earlier $4 billion paid to settle a criminal investigation, an estimated $10.3 billion to settle several civil cases, and an undetermined amount the company will need to settle future civil cases (around 3,000 such cases).[28]

The Key Decision-Making Challenge:
The Gap between the Strategy Pillar and
the Law Pillar

The following diagram depicts the expanded version of the Harvard model in which economics is replaced by strategy:

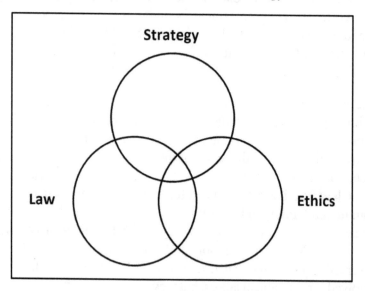

This revised model—with its sweet spot in the middle—might be more aspirational than descriptive of the overlap among the Three Pillars. True, the overlap between the Strategy Pillar and the Ethics Pillar has increased in recent years, especially as more companies embrace corporate social responsibility. For example, in discussing what they call the "intertwined nature of business and ethical interests,"[29] Bagley et al. note that former Johnson & Johnson CEO Ralph Larson was asked whether he wanted the company "to maximize shareholder value or be a good corporate citizen." He answered "Yes."

Law and ethics are even more intertwined than strategy and ethics. Legal doctrines such as fraud, unconscionability, good faith, and fiduciary duty provide solid guidelines for ethical conduct. Ben W. Heineman, former senior vice president of General Electric Company, succinctly noted two key decision-making questions: "Is it legal?" and "Is it right?"[30] Furthermore, company "codes of conduct" often blend law and ethics.

However, a gap often exists between the Strategy and Law Pillars. For reasons discussed later, strategy and law are often engaged in parallel play with the result that, in practice, the model often looks like this.

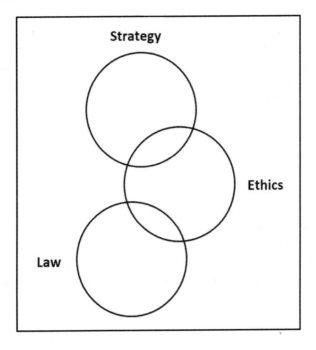

For example, the multitude of strategy concepts and frameworks that have developed over the years provide little explicit mention of law. A notable exception is a PESTLE analysis, which scans the external environment of business through the lens of six factors: **P**olitical, **E**conomic, **S**ocial, **T**echnological, **L**egal, and **E**nvironmental. The legal factor in this analysis focuses on the legal concerns that impact business operations and decision making.

Other models implicitly recognize the importance of the Law Pillar. For example, Professor Bagley in her book *Winning Legally* (2005) and Richard Shell (the Thomas Gerrity Professor in the Legal Studies and Business Ethics Department at Wharton) in his book *Make the Rules or Your Rivals Will* (2004) analyze how the law affects each of Michael Porter's aforementioned five forces.

But in practice, it is difficult for business leaders to bridge the gap between law and strategy. This difficulty arises from the mysterious nature of the Law Pillar, which is the product of the complexity of law and misconceptions about the role of lawyers. This section will explore these two factors—complexity and misconceptions—in greater detail. The next section will then describe how businesses can create a sweet spot by closing the gap between the Strategy Pillar and the Law Pillar. While Harvard calls this sweet spot the zone of sustainability, for reasons described later a more precise name is the "zone of sustainable competitive advantage."

Complexity of Law

Over the years, I have taught in many executive programs designed for business decision-makers ranging from newly-appointed managers to CEOs. One takeaway from this experience is that they feel frustrated when making law-related business decisions. This frustration results in large part from not understanding the branches that form the basic structure of the Law Pillar and the many fields emanating from these branches. The main branches are represented by the following simplified roadmap of the law.

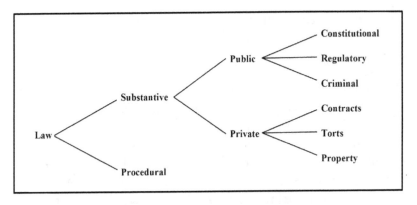

The labels for the roadmap's two main branches, substantive law and procedural law, are descriptive. Substantive law refers to the substance of the law—the legal rules that govern business operations and decision-making. Procedural law refers to the procedures used to enforce substantive law. For example, procedural law deals with how cases are filed and appealed and the rules of evidence that are used during trials.

Substantive law is primarily a concern of business decision-makers, whereas procedural law is a main concern of lawyers. But in recent years, business leaders have also become interested in procedural law—in the guise of alternative dispute resolution ("ADR"). Business leaders' interest in ADR arose in the latter half of the 20th century when they began to question why they outsourced their disputes to the court system, often at great cost in time and money. Chapter 7 of this book includes a review of ADR concepts and management tools.

Substantive law branches into public law and private law. Public law includes areas of law where the government plays a key role. The constitutional law branch focuses on the basic legal principles that govern society and the organization of government into executive, legislative, and judicial functions. Regulatory law—an area of law especially important to business that is covered in Chapter 4—encompasses the work of governmental agencies that exercise all three functions. Criminal law involves cases brought by a public official asserting that a defendant has committed a crime.

Private law includes areas of law that involve, for the most part, individuals and private entities. (Private law is also called civil law, but "civil" has other meanings in the law. For example, it is used to distinguish criminal from noncriminal cases and to distinguish common law systems that originated in England from civil systems that originated in continental Europe.) There are three main categories of private law. Contract law (covered in Chapter 6) deals with creating and enforcing legal agreements. Tort law (Chapter 2) involves a wrongful act that injures a person or property. Property law (Chapter 5) focuses on the right to own and use property.

Six of the endpoints in the roadmap—constitutional, criminal, contracts, torts, property, and procedure—are the core subjects that students study in law schools worldwide. A law student's brain is molded to think in these categories. As a result, when you pose a question to a lawyer, the answer will usually consider one or more of these six main branches along with many related fields. Wikipedia, for instance, lists more than 100 areas of law study and practice.[31] The complexity of a lawyer's advice is often amplified when the business is engaged in global transactions.

Employment law illustrates the branches of law that managers must consider when making business decisions. Employment law touches everyone in business, from entrepreneurs hiring their first employees to CEOs managing large corporations. This area of law, which brings into play all of the main branches of public and private law, includes collective bargaining agreements, discrimination, employee benefits, health and safety, hiring and firing, work hours, and pay.

These fields continually evolve and change. As noted in Siedel et al., *Employers and the Law* (2014), current topics include "Bring Your Own Device" policies (relating to using your personal smartphone at work), bullying, lactation discrimination, obesity, retaliation, and workplace violence.

Misconceptions about the Role of Lawyers

In addition to its complexity, the Law Pillar is mysterious because misconceptions abound about the role of lawyers. Media headlines contribute to confusion when they focus on contentious civil and criminal trials that have the potential to destroy companies and careers.

The media-created perception that lawyers are mainly litigators is especially misleading given that the number of cases that go to trial has dropped dramatically in recent years. In the mid-20th century (1962), more than 11% of federal civil cases reached trial; by 2002, that number dropped to less than 2%.[32]

The real day-to-day legal issues are often overlooked because they are buried in articles that focus on business transactions, not conflict. And there are many of these articles. A study by Lee Reed (Emeritus Professor of Legal Studies and former holder of the Scherer Chair at the University of Georgia's Terry College of Business) concluded that during a randomly selected month, almost half of the articles on the front pages of Sections A and B and on the editorial page of the *Wall Street Journal* focused on a legal issue or on law-related subject matter.[33]

To effectively use legal advice, managers should understand that a lawyer's role in business involves much more than litigation. From a big picture perspective, lawyers serve two functions that are critical to business success.

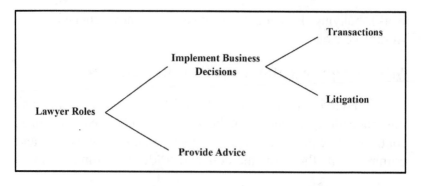

First, they serve an advisory role. Virtually every important business decision includes legal questions and requires legal advice. Second, they serve an implementation role that has two branches. If a business decision results in litigation, lawyers manage the litigation process and advise the managers who are responsible for making settlement decisions. If the business decision requires transactional work, they assist managers with the transaction—creating a joint venture, meeting regulatory requirements, acquiring real estate, creating a contract, completing a merger, developing a pension plan, and so on. To use the terminology of Ronald Gilson (Marc and Eva Stern Professor of Law and Business at Columbia University) lawyers are "transaction cost engineers" tasked with developing efficient mechanisms that create value.[34]

Transaction cost engineering is an example of what Michael Porter calls operational effectiveness, which he defines as "performing similar activities *better* than rivals perform them."[35] The problem with focusing on operational effectiveness, he notes, is that "Competitors can quickly imitate management techniques, new technologies, input improvements, and superior ways of meeting customers' needs." Consequently, business leaders should define the value added by their lawyers more broadly, with a focus on risk management.

In providing advice and assisting business leaders with their transactional and litigation decisions, lawyers themselves often view managing risk as their *raison d'étre*. As a result, although transaction cost engineering is an important part of their transactional work, a more accurate job description that encompasses all aspects of a lawyer's advisory and implementation functions is "risk management engineer."

As Gilson himself notes: "When my question—what does a business lawyer really do—is put to business lawyers, the familiar response is that they 'protect' their clients, that they get their clients the 'best' deal."[36] The president of Booz Allen Hamilton recently observed that his lawyer "is the person who is charged with protecting the corporation and making sure risks are understood and managed appropriately."[37]

A major Association of Corporate Counsel ("ACC")/Georgetown report on the role of general counsel concluded that both general counsel and company directors think that the value of strategic input from general counsel will increase in the future. But to develop their skills as strategic thinkers, lawyers "need to be comfortable with risk and helping their business colleagues decide which risks are reasonable and which are not."[38]

The link between risk management and value creation is not new. Joan Gabel, provost at the University of South Carolina and former DeSantis Professor of Legal Studies at Florida State's College of Business, has observed that historically there have examples of opportunities that were created by legal protection. This can result in what she notes is a "huge competitive advantage...."[39]

Understanding legal risk management is especially important to business leaders because legal risk is the most important category of business risk. This is reflected in the latest Travelers Business Risk Index developed from a survey of more than 1200 business risk managers representing ten industries. The managers were questioned about their greatest risk concerns among several categories, including financial, operational, and legal risk. Only two categories—"Legal Liability" and "Medical Cost Inflation"—were among the top ten risks in every industry. Another category of legal risk, "Complying with Laws," was in the top ten list for nine of the ten industries.[40]

An Accenture survey of C-suite executives (CEOs, CFOs, etc.) spread across seven industry groups in Asia Pacific, Europe, Latin America, and North America concluded that "Legal Risks" constitute the top external pressure faced by business, well ahead of the second and third risks—"Business Risks" and "Regulatory Requirements."[41]

Other studies describe the specific types of risks that concern business. The 2015 Norton Rose Fulbright survey of litigation trends in twenty-six countries listed the most common types of litigation, including the percentage of companies affected by each type of litigation.[42]

- Contracts (38%)
- Labor/Employment (37%)
- Regulatory/Investigations (18%)
- Personal Injury and Product Liability (15% and 11%, respectively)
- Intellectual Property/Patents (13%)
- Dispute Resolution Process—i.e., Class Actions (10%)

Another recent survey, by AlixPartners, concluded that the top three categories of the most common types of litigation (which clearly outdistanced the other types of litigation) are Contract, Employment, and Intellectual Property/Patent. The respondents were compliance and legal officers from companies representing more than 20 industries. Eight percent of the respondents reported that they had "been involved in a 'bet the company' lawsuit during the prior 12 months." Half of these "bet the company" lawsuits were contract disputes and 38% involved intellectual property.[43]

Yet another recent study, a global survey by Berwin Leighton Paisner, concluded that 80% of respondents (C-suite executives from a variety of sectors) "expected their business to experience material losses as a result of legal risks."[44] According to this survey the top three legal risk priorities are (in order of priority) legislation/regulation, dispute management, and contractual risk.

Regulation also tops the list of concerns in two other recent surveys. An EY survey of Chief Operating Officers and heads of investment operations in the Americas and Europe concluded that their top challenge (by a wide margin) is compliance with regulatory requirements.[45] And the 2016 PwC Annual Global CEO Survey concluded that "Over-regulation remains the top concern for business...."[46] According to Robert Bird (the Eversource Energy Chair in Business Ethics in the Business Law Department at the University of Connecticut School of Business) and Janine Hiller (a business law professor who is the Sorenson Professor of Finance at Virginia Tech's Pamplin School of Business), "A blossoming risk management industry has driven the need for positions in contract and regulatory risk management."[47]

One implication of these surveys and studies is that legal risk has a major impact on a company's bottom line. As noted by Henry Lowenstein (former Dean at California State University at Bakersfield and currently a business law professor at Coastal Carolina University, where he holds the Baxley Professorship), "As a practical matter for businesses today, the legal expense line is now a significant factor on company balance sheets."[48]

When working with lawyers on the legal issues that dominate business risk management, business leaders should understand whom the lawyer represents and the lawyer's duty to provide independent professional judgement, along with related attorney-client privilege concerns. As noted in the ACC/Georgetown study on the role of general counsel, lawyers face a continuing challenge in maintaining "professional independence and recognizing the organization as a client, as opposed to the CEO or other members of the C-suite...."[49]

The independence issue becomes complicated in a global economy because an in-house lawyer's duty of independence varies from country to country, with repercussions on attorney-client privilege. But even when independence is not legally required, obtaining and understanding independent professional advice is especially important to business leaders. Providing this advice often requires managerial courage on the lawyer's part. As defined by the ACC/Georgetown study, "Managerial courage is about the willingness and ability to speak up and represent the organization and act in its best interest, even when it feels uncomfortable or may reflect poorly on colleagues."[50] Exercising such courage can serve as a valuable antidote to a manager's confirmation bias—the tendency to rely only on evidence that confirms a decision the manager wants to make.[51]

The combination of a risk management focus and independence often causes tension among lawyers and business decision makers. A participant in one of my executive programs told me that in his company the law department is secretly called the "department of sales prevention." Other managers refer to the law function as the "department of no," in contrast to IT and other "departments of now" that need legal information as quickly as possible.[52] Despite this tension, the lawyers' focus on risk management enables business leaders to balance an unbridled emphasis on shareholder value creation represented by the Strategy Pillar with managing risks represented by the Law Pillar.

Although a focus on both reward and risk is necessary, business leaders miss opportunities when the Strategy Pillar and the Law Pillar run on separate tracks that do not intersect. In the next section, we examine how the gap between these two key elements in business decision making can be closed in a manner that enhances the opportunity for business success.

Closing the Gap Between Strategy and Law

The gap between the Strategy Pillar and the Law Pillar is reminiscent of the "mind the gap" recording that one hears when traveling on the London Underground and elsewhere. While minding the gap—that is, understanding that the gap exists—is important, deciding what action to take after you are warned of the gap is essential. This section focuses on *how* to mind the gap.

How large is this gap? The Berwin Leighton survey mentioned earlier concluded that most board-level respondents felt that their firms do not use "legal-risk reports to inform strategic, risk-based business decisions."[53] But the strategy–law gap is not all bad news for companies such as Microsoft that are able to close the gap successfully. According to a Microsoft attorney, "the business strategy is developed in close cooperation with Legal and Corporate Affairs—it's not a business strategy and then the legal strategy, it's a common strategy...."[54]

By closing the gap, companies using the Microsoft approach have an opportunity to create competitive advantage over their rivals. According to University of Connecticut Professor Robert Bird, when this happens the competitive advantage can be sustainable. In other words, the sweet spot in decision-making that Harvard calls the zone of sustainability might be more accurately described as the zone of sustainable competitive advantage.[55]

Bird's conclusion is based on a legal analysis using a resource attribute framework developed by strategy professor Jay Barney. One takeaway from this analysis is that law's complexity is a factor in creating a resource that, in Barney's language, is imperfectly imitable by competitors. In other words, managers who are able to penetrate the veil of complexity and mystery that surrounds the law have an opportunity to create a sustainable competitive advantage.

31

Bird and coauthor David Orozco (a business law professor and the Dean's Emerging Scholar at Florida State University's College of Business) describe various pathways of corporate legal strategy in a recent article in the *MIT Sloan Management Review*.[56] They emphasize the need for "a fundamental change from managing risk to creating business opportunities" that requires business leaders to "possess legal astuteness and regard the law as a key enabler of value creation." In her book *Winning Legally* (2005), Professor Bagley was a pioneer in recognizing legal astuteness as a key element in a manager's skill set.

The next section discusses how you can become legally savvy (that is, legally astute). We then turn to how you can use your understanding of the law to close the gap between the Strategy Pillar and the Law Pillar through a reframing process.

Becoming a Legally Savvy Business Leader

A business leader who is savvy has a practical understanding of the realities of law and business. Many people in business lack the legal savvy necessary to bridge the gap between managing risk and creating value. For example, the aforementioned Berwin Leighton survey concluded that only 25% of the directors and CEOs surveyed had a clear understanding of legal risk.[57]

The need to become legally savvy is obviously important for business leaders tasked with establishing a company's strategic direction. But middle managers who implement strategy also play an important role in legal decision-making. A recent Corporate Executive Board Legal Leadership Council survey concluded that middle managers make 75% of legal decisions and that almost "80% of corporate employees made a decision or completed an activity with a significant legal implication in the past year."[58]

These middle-management decisions involved, for example, signing contracts, developing new products, creating intellectual property, interacting with government officials, entering a new market, creating marketing materials, establishing product safety standards, and executing an acquisition agreement. Less than one-third of these middle managers consulted the legal department when making their decisions. In other words, they relied on their own knowledge of the law when making business decisions that were rife with legal concerns.

How does someone become a legally savvy business leader? Three common options are (1) learn on the job, (2) attend law school, or (3) take business law courses in business school. Learning on the job is challenging and risky because, without a foundational understanding of legal concepts and frameworks, it is difficult for a manager to decide when to seek legal advice and how to communicate effectively with a lawyer. These difficulties might account for the large number of aforementioned "bet the company" lawsuits that are in progress. Even when company survival is not at stake, litigation is an expensive and time-consuming learning process.

Law schools and business schools are the best option to become legally savvy. They also have a comparative advantage in teaching the law. An essay by University of Chicago Professor James Lorie on the Chicago model of education emphasized the key business-related areas best suited for business school instruction. In his words, a university "has its greatest advantage in teaching such basic disciplines as mathematics, statistics, accounting, economics, law, psychology, and sociology; it has least competence in teaching the current practice, techniques, and language of business."[59]

Law School Option. Outside the United States, majoring in law is an alternative to business school for individuals planning a career in management. And even in the United States, where the study of law tends to be professionalized, law school can be an entry point into a business career. As Bagley et al. note, in the early years of the 20th century, more than 75% of US CEOs had a legal background.

Although legal study provides valuable knowledge about details of the law, other benefits are especially useful in a business career, such as developing critical thinking and communication skills, the ability to think logically, understanding how to prevent and resolve business disputes, an ability to evaluate global legal trends that impact business, and understanding a business leader's legal responsibilities.

When combined with a business degree, a law degree can provide an especially solid foundation for a successful business career. For example, many graduates of the Ross School of Business at the University of Michigan have also graduated from law school. These graduates include several leading University of Michigan benefactors, such as Stephen Ross (gifts of more than $310 million), Sam Zell (gifts of $225 million) and the late William Davidson (gifts of $55 million).

Business School Option. The problem with the law school option for becoming legally savvy is that the time (in the United States three years of graduate study) and expense can exceed the benefits for someone who does not intend to practice law. So the option of taking business law courses while pursuing a business degree is the most cost-effective approach. Recognizing the importance of these courses, the AACSB (the accrediting body for business schools) has adopted an international accreditation standard that states an expectation that business school degree programs will cover the legal context of organizations. As Jeffrey Garten, former dean of the Yale School of Management, has noted: "All students… should gain a fundamental understanding of business law."[60]

On a general level, this "fundamental understanding" includes the study of the interaction between business and society. A leading book on undergraduate education, for instance, concluded that business law courses, more than any other business school area of study, "help prepare students for the complexity of roles demanded by the modern business enterprise."[61] On a specific level, the "fundamental understanding" includes the most important legal concerns that managers must understand, as listed in the surveys described earlier: contracts, employment law, government regulation, tort law, intellectual property, and the legal process.

But just as important as these areas of law are the skills that enable you to make decisions in a legally savvy manner. In addition to the general legal skills that result from the study of law (such as critical thinking skills, understanding how to prevent and resolve business disputes, and an ability to evaluate global legal trends that impact business), business law courses provide graduates with these seven management skills that are essential to success in business:

1. **The ability to recognize the legal issues that arise on a daily basis in business.** In her book *Winning Legally* (2005), Bagley noted that businesses swim "in a sea of law." A director at Royal Dutch Shell confirmed this perspective with this story:

    > Two young fish swim along and happen to meet an older fish swimming the other way, who nods at them and says, "Morning, boys. How's the water?" The two young fish swim on for a bit, until, eventually, one of them looks over at the other and goes, "What the hell is water?" Like water, law is around us—everywhere. It affects everything a company does. But somehow you can't see it, at least not on the surface.[62]

    Business graduates should have the ability to recognize the legal issues that lurk beneath the surface of the legal sea in which they swim.

2. **The ability to decide which legal issues require you to seek professional advice.** Having a lawyer at your elbow to provide advice on the myriad legal issues you face daily is not feasible in terms of time and expense. You must address most of these issues on your own, in effect acting as your own lawyer. But you also must be able to decide which of your daily issues are serious enough to require legal counsel so that you can make sound business decisions and avoid litigation, especially the "bet the company" litigation that so many companies face today.

3. **The ability to communicate effectively with lawyers when you seek their advice.** Effective communication begins with you placing the legal issue in perspective using the legal roadmap depicted earlier. Communication also requires a fundamental understanding of the main branches in the roadmap, because they reflect the key legal concerns that companies today face.

4. **The ability to evaluate the advice an attorney provides.** The responsibility for deciding when and how to take legal risks when making business decisions falls on you, not your attorney. In exercising this responsibility, you often must balance legal advice with recommendations from others in the business. For example, when the media contacts you after someone has been injured by your product, your attorney might suggest that you not comment—or at least not apologize—while your public relations advisor might recommend the opposite. The decision is yours.

5. **The ability to implement the legal decisions that you make.** Using the same example, you must decide what to say and how to say it when meeting with the media.

6. **The ability to discuss legal issues with stakeholders.** As a business leader—whether an entrepreneur operating a start-up or the head of a major corporation—you are (in effect, if not in title) the "Chief Legal Communicator" in discussing legal concerns with company shareholders, employees, customers, government regulators, suppliers, and other stakeholders.

7. **The ability to exercise leadership in emphasizing legal responsibilities to everyone in your organization.** As noted previously, many of the costly decision-making blunders that the media loosely calls "ethical lapses" are in fact violations of the law. You must ensure that all employees understand their legal responsibilities.

Reframing the Strategy Pillar and the Law Pillar: A Trip to the Balcony

Becoming a legally-savvy business leader is necessary but not sufficient for business success. The problem is that, even if you understand the law, the Strategy Pillar and the Law Pillar often operate as separate silos where key business questions are framed in terms of either shareholder value or risk management, either reward or risk.

At best, this parallel play is unfortunate because you will miss opportunities to create value through synergies between strategy and law. At worst, the silo mentality is destructive when it creates a conflict between the Strategy Pillar and the Law Pillar—for example, when a risk-averse approach results in an overly legalistic contract that destroys a business opportunity. In the words of PepsiCo CEO Indra Nooyi when commenting on the combination of a perfect contract with a flawed business deal, "We cannot afford this separation of church and state."[63]

An important cause of this silo mentality is what decision researchers call frame blindness. Mental frames are often useful because they enable us to simplify and organize our world's complexity so that we can make rational decisions. But simplification can come at a cost. When we view the world through a particular window—from the perspective of the Strategy Pillar or the Legal Pillar, for example— we see only part of the landscape. Narrowing the scope of our vision causes us to become susceptible to frame blindness—think of it as the blind spot on the side-view mirrors of your car. By failing to consider the big picture, we often miss the best options when making decisions.[64]

For example, I give my students an exercise in which they play the role of a business leader who must decide whether to accept a settlement offer from the opposing side in a lawsuit. Almost all of the students exhibit frame blindness by concentrating on the legal issues raised in the case. In so doing, they overlook fundamental finance and strategy concerns, such as the net present value of the litigation, opportunity costs, and the possibility of creating a joint venture with the other side.

Closing the gap between strategy and law requires reducing frame blindness by reframing the shareholder value orientation that characterizes the Strategy Pillar and the risk management orientation that dominates the Law Pillar. A major challenge that inhibits reframing is what Max Bazerman and Don Moore call the "fixed-pie assumption" that is often made during negotiations.[65]

Bazerman and Moore observe that this assumption is a fundamental bias that distorts negotiators' behavior as they fight over what they think is a fixed pie: "When negotiating over an issue, they [negotiators] assume that their interests necessarily and directly conflict with the other party's interests." By identifying interests that are not in conflict, business decision-makers (such as negotiators) have an opportunity to expand the pie so that it benefits the company and its stakeholders.[66]

Management decisions within the Law Pillar can be especially susceptible to fixed-pie thinking, because litigation is typically a zero sum game where one side wins and the other side loses. But the fixed-pie assumption also impacts decisions within the Strategy Pillar when decision-makers assume that a gain for some stakeholders must necessarily result in a loss for shareholders.

A View from the Balcony. Avoiding frame blindness and fixed-pie thinking requires a big-picture mindset. In his book *Getting Past No* (1993), William Ury uses the phrase "going to the balcony" as a metaphor to describe the mental detachment often necessary to create this mindset. From the balcony you have the opportunity to gain a broad perspective that allows you to see the entire playing field without the blind spots that hinder decision-making when you are closer to the action.

Especially important in your view from the balcony is realizing that the playing field of business includes many key stakeholders (in addition to shareholders) who impact your business success. Which stakeholders have the greatest effect on a company's economic value? A McKinsey survey that posed this question produced responses from 1,396 executives worldwide. Respondents were allowed to select multiple responses from a list of stakeholders. The dominant four stakeholders match the constituents emphasized in the Harvard course described earlier. Three-quarters of the executives felt that customers had the greatest effect on economic value. The other main categories were government/regulators (53%), employees (49%), and investors (28%).[67]

Viewing the business playing field from the balcony enables you to reframe your fixed-pie mindset by considering these stakeholder interests—interests that might be aligned with your company's financial success. Just as the most successful negotiators have the ability to look at deals from the opposing side's perspective, you should look at your value creation and risk management decisions from the perspective of all stakeholders affected by your decisions.

What are these stakeholder interests? How can you link these interests to company interests to create a larger pie that benefits all parties?

By addressing these questions, you can move beyond the shareholder value/frame blindness of the Strategy Pillar and the value protection/frame blindness of the Law Pillar to a joint interest-based mindset. This new mindset creates an overlap of the Strategy Pillar and the Law Pillar that has the potential to benefit all parties, while creating competitive advantage for your company.

Moving beyond the fixed-pie assumption is consistent with a relatively new approach called the Proactive Law Movement, which originated in Europe. Under the leadership of my frequent coauthor Helena Haapio, an International Contract Counsel for Lexpert, Ltd, this movement focuses on using the law not only to manage risk, but also to create value and strengthen relationships.[68] Haapio's pioneering work on contract visualization will be described later in this book. Several scholars in the United States have written on proactive law, including Larry DiMatteo (Huber Hurst Professor of Contract Law and Legal Studies at the University of Florida's Warrington College of Business), with whom Haapio and I authored a chapter in the book *Proactive Law in a Business Environment*.[69]

Michael Porter and Mark Kramer in "Creating Shared Value" advocate in part a management philosophy similar to the interest-based approach to management decisions.[70] They redefine the purpose of the corporation as "creating shared value, not just profit per se." But unlike the interest-based approach described here, their shared-value philosophy focuses primarily on one stakeholder—society. In their words, the principle of shared value "involves creating economic value in a way that also creates value for society by addressing its needs and challenges." An interest-based strategy, in contrast, searches for value-creating opportunities for all dominant stakeholders identified in the McKinsey survey—customers, the government, employees, and investors.

The Legality of an Interest-Based Approach to Bridge the Strategy–Law Gap. An interest-based approach faces an important challenge relating to the legal purpose of a corporation: Does the law require business leaders to give primacy to shareholder value? Or said differently, isn't the legal purpose of a corporation to create shareholder value? If the answer to these questions is "yes" then an interest-based model, especially one that might benefit other stakeholders more than shareholders, is legally suspect.

The Michigan Supreme Court discussed these questions in an iconic case, *Dodge v. Ford Motor Co.* (1919). Two shareholders of the Ford Motor Company, Horace and John Dodge (who owned 10% of the stock) claimed that the company should pay shareholders a dividend beyond the regular dividend of 60% per year. Among other things, they wanted the court to order the company to pay shareholders 75% of the accumulated cash surplus of over $50 million.

Henry Ford dominated the company, holding 58% of the company's stock. He wanted to plow most of the profits back into the company so that he could expand the business and (as he was quoted by the court) "employ still more men; to spread the benefits of this industrial system to the greatest possible number, to help them build up their lives and their homes." During the trial Ford elaborated on these goals when answering questions posed by the Dodge brothers' lawyer, Elliott Stevenson. Here is an excerpt from the trial transcript, which begins with the lawyer asking Ford about a newspaper interview in which Ford apologized for making an "awful profit" on car sales:[71]

> *Stevenson*: I will ask you again, do you still think those profits were "awful profits?"

Ford: Well, I guess I do, yes.

Stevenson: And for that reason you were not satisfied to continue to make such "awful profits?"

Ford: We don't seem to be able to keep the profits down.

Stevenson: [A]re you trying to keep them down? What is the Ford Motor Company organized for except profits, will you tell me, Mr. Ford?

Ford: Organized to do as much good as we can, everywhere, for everybody concerned.

Stevenson: What is the purpose of the company?

Ford: To do as much as possible for everybody concerned…. To make money and use it, give employment, and send out the car where the people can use it…. [A]nd incidentally to make money.

Stevenson: Incidentally make money?

Ford: Yes, sir.

Stevenson: But your controlling feature, so far as your policy… is to employ a great army of men at high wages, to reduce the selling price of your car, so that a lot of people can buy it at a cheap price, and give everybody a car that wants one?

Ford: If you give all that, the money will fall into your hands; you can't get out of it.

This case raises questions about the legal purpose of a corporation. Deciding the case in favor of the Dodge brothers (on grounds that withholding the dividends was a breach of duty to shareholders), the court's comments could be construed as a rallying cry for advocates of shareholder primacy: "A business corporation is organized and carried on primarily for the profit of the stockholders." The court qualified this statement by noting that corporations can make humanitarian expenditures to benefit employees (such as building a hospital) but cannot operate for the primary purpose of benefitting others.

The court's statement aligns with the views of Nobel Prize-winning economist Milton Friedman and other proponents of shareholder primacy, including those who believe that the *Dodge* court's opinion states a legal requirement. These proponents overlook the fact that the statement is not law because the court was merely stating an opinion (called *dicta*) that was not essential to its decision. And, as iconoclast Lynn Stout (the Distinguished Professor of Corporate & Business Law at Cornell University) has observed, other sources of law also do not require maximizing shareholder wealth. To the contrary, "A large majority of state codes contain so-called other-constituency provisions that explicitly authorize corporate boards to consider the interests of not just shareholders, but also employees, customers, creditors, and the community, in making business decisions."[72]

So the bottom line is that the law does not prevent a trip to the balcony to consider the interests of stakeholders beyond shareholders. As Chapter 8 will explain, this interest-based approach, in addition to linking the Strategy Pillar to the Law Pillar, enables you to establish values that can guide decisions within the Ethics Pillar.

These values are especially important in today's business environment. According to a recent KPMG survey (with more than 3,500 respondents from a wide variety of industries), 73% of employees had observed misconduct in the workplace. Most of this misconduct (reported by 56% of respondents) was serious— "possibly resulting in a significant loss of public trust." The most commonly cited cause of misconduct is "pressure to do 'whatever it takes' to meet business goals," coupled with a belief that company codes of conduct are not taken seriously.[73]

One problem with codes of conduct is that companies use a top-down approach when creating them. This approach ignores the reality that "executives cannot just descend from some ethical mountaintop with a couple of stone tablets and expect immediate compliance."[74] In contrast, standards of conduct that are linked to the Strategy Pillar and the Law Pillar become automatically embedded in everyday decision-making.

The ability to consider the interests of constituents other than shareholders is especially important given the recent surge in interest in creating companies that seek profits for their shareholders while simultaneously serving the interests of other stakeholders. The late C.K. Prahalad, a renowned strategy professor at the Ross School of Business, was influential in creating this interest with his best-selling book *Fortune at the Bottom of the Pyramid: Eradicating Poverty Through Profits* (2006). Today, "profits with a purpose" has become the theme for a new generation of business leaders. As noted by Professor Shawn Cole, who teaches a course on "Business at the Base of the Pyramid" at Harvard Business School, "There's often an alignment between personal enrichment and improving the wealth of others. Students see a real opportunity here."[75]

The Three Pillars Mantra

To summarize this chapter, business decisions are made within the Three Pillar framework. The major challenge in using the model is the gap between the Strategy Pillar and the Law Pillar. Closing this gap enables businesses to create a sweet spot at the intersection of the Three Pillars—the zone of sustainable competitive advantage.

Regardless of whether you are starting your own business or making decisions within a large organization, the key to closing the gap is for you to become a legally savvy decision maker. This will enable you to understand the Law Pillar and manage the legal risks associated with your strategic plan. Becoming legally savvy will also allow you to ascend the balcony to reframe your decisions relating to creating shareholder value (Strategy Pillar) and managing risk (Law Pillar). As part of the reframing process, you should consider the interests of all stakeholders and try to develop opportunities for mutual value creation.

In shorthand, your mantra should be Understand, Protect, and Create. You should *understand* the Law Pillar, *protect* your company through legal risk management, and *create* value with an interest-based mindset that results in a larger pie for the company and its stakeholders.

The Organization of this Book

The aforementioned McKinsey survey noted that the four key business stakeholders are:

1.   Customers
2.   Employees
3.   The Government
4.   Investors

Other surveys have concluded that the top risks affecting companies are:

1.   Tort law (including Product Liability)
2.   Employment Law
3.   Regulatory Law
4.   Intellectual Property Law
5.   Contracts
6.   Dispute Resolution

This book links the four key stakeholders to the first four risks. This structure enables you to become legally savvy about these risks while at the same time understanding how to manage them and create value for your stakeholders. For example, Chapter 2 links the first stakeholder (your customers) to the first risk (tort and product liability law—a major risk for business). This chapter, titled "Meet Your Customers' Needs: Transform Product Liability into Product Innovation," includes these elements:

- **Legal briefing:** The features of tort and product liability law that every business decision maker should understand to become legally savvy
- **Risk management:** Business strategies and solutions to minimize product liability
- **Interest-based value creation:** Aligning the Strategy Pillar with the Law Pillar to create value for stakeholders
- **Key takeaways:** An executive summary of the chapter

Chapters 3 through 5 link the other three stakeholders—employees, the government and investors—with areas of the law that are especially relevant to them:

- Chapter 3: Use Employment Law to Attract and Retain the Best Business Talent
- Chapter 4: Use Government Regulation to Develop New Business Models
- Chapter 5: Use Your Intellectual Property to Create Shareholder Value

Chapters 6 and 7 address the final two significant business risks identified by surveys of business leaders: contract and dispute resolution processes. Understanding these processes is especially important because they affect all stakeholders.

- Chapter 6: Develop Contracts that Create Value for Both Sides
- Chapter 7: Use Dispute Resolution Processes for Value Creation

Like Chapter 2, Chapters 3–7 include these features: a legal briefing, risk management to minimize your liability, a trip to the balcony to engage in interest-based value creation, and Key Takeaways. In some cases, the balcony perspective even provides ideas for new business models based on opportunities the law creates. An example is Chapter 4's coverage of the Regulatory Gap Strategy, which has been used by companies like Southwest Airlines and Uber.

Chapter 8, the final chapter, focuses on how to create and lead an ethical business. As an ethical business leader you should understand

- how the law influences ethical decision making within your company,
- the elements that your company should include in its compliance program and code of conduct,
- how you can set high standards as an ethical leader in your business, and
- how your business can meet societal needs while also creating value for shareholders.

These topics are covered in Chapter 8, where the focus in on creating both value and values.

The ultimate goal of this book is to enable you to make decisions that minimize your legal risks while creating value for your business and its stakeholders. My hope is that your ability to use the Three Pillar model when making business decisions will also add value when making decisions in other areas of your life—even when ordering the pizza described in the opening of this chapter.

II UNDERSTAND HOW TO MANAGE KEY BUSINESS STAKEHOLDER RISKS WHILE CREATING VALUE

2 Meet Your Customers' Needs: Transform Product Liability into Product Innovation

This chapter examines a key business risk, product liability, as it relates to your customers. As noted in Chapter 1, a McKinsey survey of stakeholders showed that customers have the most significant effect on a company's economic value. Other studies have identified torts, in general, and product liability, specifically, as key risks to a company's success.

This chapter opens with an overview of product liability and its impact on customers, companies, and society. The second section provides a legal briefing on tort law and product liability, which is designed to help you become legally savvy about these important topics. The third section covers risk management—that is, how you can minimize product liability (which is the key focus of the Law Pillar of decision making). The final section merges the Law Pillar and Strategy Pillar by showing how even a contentious area of law like product liability can be used to create value for businesses by focusing on customer interests.

Impact of Product Liability

Product liability is an especially controversial topic because of its impact on companies, customers, and society in general.

Impact of Product Liability on Companies

Product liability as we know it today is the result of changes in the law over the last third of the 20th century. These changes left in their wake the bankruptcy of a large number of companies, including industrial giants such as Johns Manville Corporation, A. H. Robins Co., and Dow Corning Corp. Product liability is often front page news as companies manufacturing cars, drugs, tobacco and a variety of other products face lawsuits where claims can exceed billions of dollars.

Less well publicized is the impact of product liability on smaller companies that are forced out of business because they cannot compete effectively while paying high product liability insurance premiums. Few people know about Havir Manufacturing, a small punch press manufacturer that was based in St. Paul, Minnesota several years ago. Havir was doing fine until, in one year, its product liability insurance premium jumped 1900%, which equaled 10% of the company's sales. The company could not afford to stay in business, so it auctioned off its equipment and laid off its workers.[1]

Impact of Product Liability on Consumers

From a consumer perspective, product liability forces companies to act responsibly in manufacturing and selling products. The size of jury awards often reflects the consumer perspective. For example, Patricia Anderson purchased a used Chevrolet Malibu. While she was driving home from a Christmas Eve church service with her four children, a speeding drunk driver rear-ended her vehicle. Anderson escaped serious injury, but the four children, who were sitting in the back seat, were horribly disfigured when the gas tank erupted in flames.

Anderson sued General Motors ("GM"), and a jury held the company liable for $107 million in compensatory damages and another $4.8

billion in punitive damages. A judge later ruled that the punitive damage award was excessive, and reduced the amount to "only" $1.09 billion. (GM appealed the decision and, as often happens, it is likely that the two parties reached a private settlement.)

The jury based this award in part on a finding that GM wanted to reduce costs by placing the car's gas tank under the trunk, where it was vulnerable to rupture. An internal GM memorandum concluded that placing the gas tank in a different location would cost $8.59 more per car. In another internal memorandum, a young GM engineer conducted a "value analysis," which assumed a maximum of 500 deaths per year in GM cars and a "value" (that is, the cost to GM) of $200,000 per death. Multiplying 500 times $200,000 and dividing the result by the number of GM cars on the road (41,000,000) the engineer came up with a cost per automobile of $2.40, which was less than the $8.59 cost of relocating the fuel tank.[2]

The *General Motors* case illustrates the controversial nature of product liability. Why should the company be responsible for injuries triggered by an accident that a speeding drunk driver caused? Did the engineer's memo actually influence company decisions? Did placing the gas tank under the trunk create greater danger than placement in other locations? What is the Malibu's safety record compared to other cars?

Though these are legitimate questions, it is also important to keep in mind that business leaders wear two product liability hats. In your role as a business leader, you are concerned about the impact of product liability on your company. But as a consumer, you want safe products for yourself and your loved ones.

A case in Texas illustrates these two hats. A 42-year-old attorney who specialized in defending companies in product liability cases went hunting with his 16-year-old son and two judges. After the hunt, the son entered the car holding a high-powered Remington rifle. One of the judges suggested that he unload the gun. The son released the safety, which was necessary to unload the rifle. The gun fired, wounding his father and leaving him paralyzed from the waist down. The father proceeded to sue Remington, claiming that it should not be necessary to release the safety to unload a rifle. The company paid him $6.8 million to settle the case.[3]

Impact of Product Liability on Society

Beyond the impact of product liability on individual companies and customers is the concern that product liability might inhibit innovation and new product development. Based on responses from the CEOs of 264 companies, a Conference Board study (at the time when product liability litigation first became a major problem for companies) concluded that 47% of the companies had discontinued product lines and 39% had decided not to introduce new products because of product liability. More than 40% of the CEOs indicated that product liability had a major impact on the companies' ability to compete.[4]

Legal Briefing on Tort Law and Product Liability

Understanding product liability requires some background on the fundamental nature of tort law. This section provides a legal briefing on tort law and explains how it relates to product liability.

Tort Law Fundamentals

A tort is a wrongful act that injures someone's property, body, or reputation. There are three basic types of torts: intentional torts, negligence, and strict liability.

Intentional Torts. As the name implies, intentional torts result when someone intends to cause injury. In addition to being subject to damages in a civil lawsuit, someone who commits an intentional tort might face criminal charges because intentional wrongs are both torts and crimes.

Negligence. In everyday language, negligence is carelessness that results in injury. A plaintiff who sues you for negligence must prove four key elements: (1) you owed a duty of care to the plaintiff, (2) you breached your duty of care, (3) the plaintiff suffered injury, and (4) the breach of the duty of care caused the injury.

The automobile accident is probably the most common source of tort liability worldwide. Drivers owe a duty of care to other drivers and to pedestrians. When they drive carelessly and injure someone, they breach the duty of care, and there is a causal link between this breach and the injury.

Strict Liability. In some situations there is tort liability even though the person sued did not intentionally injure someone and was not negligent. This form of liability arises when someone is engaged in an especially dangerous activity, such as housing wild animals. As discussed in the next section, in recent years, strict liability theory has been used to hold businesses liable for making and selling defective products.

Legal Elements of Product Liability

A plaintiff in a typical product liability case will assert two of the three basic tort theories—negligence and strict liability—along with breach of warranty, which is based on contract law. From a business perspective, there are three types of product defects that can lead to liability under these tort and contract theories: design defects, manufacturing defects, and marketing defects.

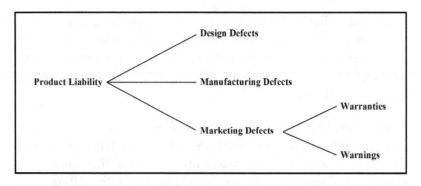

Design Defects. Your company is responsible for injuries resulting from defective product design. Your duties in designing a product are governed by reasonableness: Is the design reasonable given your customers' foreseeable uses of the product?

Courts recognize that requiring your company to develop a perfectly safe product is often unrealistic. For example, automobile manufacturers have the ability to design cars that would virtually eliminate personal injuries in automobile accidents. But what would these cars look like? Probably a lot like army tanks. These tank-like cars would be inefficient (with mileage measured in gallons to the mile rather than miles to the gallon), unattractive, prohibitively expensive, and slow. In short, no one would want to buy them.

As a result, most courts have adopted a balancing test that considers, on the one hand, the risks associated with a product, and, on the other, the benefits (or utility) of the product. The Supreme Court of Georgia summarized the balancing test in a case involving a 9-year-old child who died after eating rat poison. The poison did not contain a bitter element that would deter human consumption or cause people to vomit if they mistakenly swallowed the poison.

The court first noted that the case involved a design defect—rather than a manufacturing or marketing defect. The court then observed that the risk-utility analysis represents the "overwhelming consensus" on the law of defective design: "This risk-utility analysis incorporates the concept of 'reasonableness,' i.e., whether the manufacturer acted reasonably in choosing a particular product design, given the probability and seriousness of the risk posed by the design, the usefulness of the product in that condition, and the burden on the manufacturer to take the necessary steps to eliminate the risk."[5]

After reviewing numerous sources, the court developed a list of general factors that are considered in a risk-utility analysis. The factors, presented in question format, provide a checklist you can use when designing products:

- How useful is the product?
- Does the design create serious dangers?
- Is injury likely?
- Is the danger avoidable?
- Does the customer have an ability to avoid the danger?
- What is the state of the art (at time of manufacture)?
- Can the danger be eliminated without impairing the utility of the product or making it prohibitively expensive?
- Can the losses sustained by injured customers be spread through higher prices or insurance?
- Are alternative designs feasible, taking into account cost and adverse effects of the alternative?
- What are the benefits of the product—for example, appearance, attractiveness, usefulness for multiple purposes, and convenience?

Manufacturing Defects. Manufacturers, like other defendants, are liable for carelessness that results in injury to others (that is, negligence). Over the last half of the 20th century, American courts crafted an additional theory of liability—called strict liability—that makes it much easier for an injured consumer to win a case against a manufacturer. Under this theory, businesses that sell defective products that injure consumers are liable even if they exercise "all possible care" in preparing and selling the product. In other words, the customer no longer has to prove that the manufacturer was negligent, and the manufacturer can no longer successfully defend a lawsuit by asserting that it exercised all care humanly possible in producing the product.

Countries around the world have followed the United States in adopting the strict liability theory. Why would these countries expand traditional tort law by fashioning this rule of strict liability? One view is that the law is based on the ability of companies to pay damage awards because they have "deep pockets." Judges and legal scholars, however, claim that the law is designed to shift losses from one person (the injured consumer) to society in general. This loss-shifting occurs because of manufacturers' supposed ability to raise prices after incurring product liability costs. As one scholar observed: "[Strict liability] is not a 'deep pocket' theory but rather a 'risk-bearing economic' theory. The assumption is that the manufacturer can shift the costs of accidents to purchasers for use by charging higher prices for the costs of products."[6]

The cost-shifting aspect of product liability is illustrated by a case involving a high school student who was paralyzed when his spinal cord was severed while playing football. His lawsuit against the helmet manufacturer, Riddell, resulted in a $5.3 million judgment. Riddell's insurance company proceeded to raise the company's annual product liability insurance premiums from $40,000 to $1.5 million. Riddell responded by raising the price of helmets over the next few years by 33%, virtually all of which was attributed to product liability costs.

Football teams faced with higher helmet prices undoubtedly raised the price of tickets and advertising so that ultimately the cost fell on consumers. In other words, costs of the accident are spread among a large number of consumers rather than falling entirely on the player and his family.[7] Riddell continues to face litigation involving football injuries. In 2015, a federal judge approved the settlement of head trauma litigation brought by professional football players against the National Football League, but decided that the settlement did not apply to their claims against Riddell.[8]

One problem with strict liability theory is that many companies, unable to raise prices enough to cover product liability costs, are forced out of business. For example, the number of companies manufacturing football helmets has dropped dramatically in recent years. Companies that survive are then better able to pass on product liability costs to customers. A friend of mine who purchased a football helmet for his son in junior high school reported that a sticker on the helmet stated that one-third of the price went toward product liability costs.

Marketing Defects. Two types of marketing defects can lead to product liability. Liability can result either from express or implied warranties that your company provides to your customers or from your company's failure to warn customers of hidden dangers associated with the product.

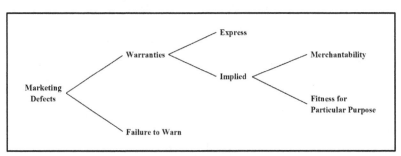

Warranties. Your warranty liability is often based on statements— called express warranties—that you make to consumers. When you state a fact, make a promise, or describe your product, you are giving express warranties. The information that you provide does not have to be distributed with the product and does not have to use the word "warranty" in order to create liability.

For example, an advertisement can create an express warranty. At one time, cigarette companies emphasized the safety of smoking with ads like the following from a US Supreme Court decision.[9] The Supreme Court ruled that a smoker could sue tobacco companies because, through these ads, cigarette companies gave express warranties that cigarettes are safe:

- Play Safe—Smoke Chesterfield
- Nose, Throat and Accessory Organs Not Adversely Affected by Smoking Chesterfields
- [Chesterfields are] entirely safe for the mouth
- [L&M filters are] Just What the Doctor Ordered

Even when your company does not give express warranties, the law automatically gives purchasers two warranties, called implied warranties. One of these implied warranties is the warranty of merchantability. With this warranty, businesses must provide products that are of average quality and fit for ordinary purposes. The other implied warranty is the warranty of fitness for a particular purpose, which applies to all sellers—even if they aren't in business. You give this warranty in situations where you know that the buyer (1) needs the product for a particular purpose and (2) is relying on your skill and judgment in providing a product that will meet the buyer's needs.

Warnings and Failure to Warn. Your company has a legal duty to warn customers about the dangers associated with the foreseeable uses of your product. This liability can arise even when products are not otherwise defective. For example, in 2013, a jury decided that Riddell was liable for $3.1 million for failing to provide an adequate warning about possible head trauma to a football player who was injured in a high school game. As a result of cases like this, helmet manufacturers have strengthened their warnings. Here is an example: "No helmet system can protect you from serious brain and/or neck injuries including paralysis or death. To avoid these risks, do not engage in the sport of football."[10]

Your company's warnings should also take into account the risk of potential psychological harm. In one case, a doctor replaced the heart valve of a patient named Bravman with a mechanical valve. The mechanical valve made a loud noise that, in some patients, could be heard in a quiet room from as far as twenty feet away. When Bravman sued the manufacturer, the court decided that there was (1) no design defect, because the product's usefulness outweighed the noise problems and (2) no manufacturing defect.

The court determined, however, that the manufacturer could be held liable for failing to warn the patient of the noise problem. Evidence surfaced that the manufacturer knew that its mechanical valves were noisy. Other patients had complained, and one patient attempted suicide because of the noise. Bravman alleged that he had lost sleep, become despondent, and been forced to take early retirement because of the noise. The court concluded that: "Unlike the purely psychological terror suffered by the protagonist in Edgar Allan Poe's The Tell-Tale Heart, Bravman's complaint, that his artificial heart valve creates excessive noise that prevents him from sleeping, among other things, is objectively verifiable."[11]

The Law Pillar: Product Liability Risk Management

Managing product liability risk to achieve competitive advantage involves three fundamental approaches: (1) a strategic approach, (2) an organizational approach, and (3) an operational approach.

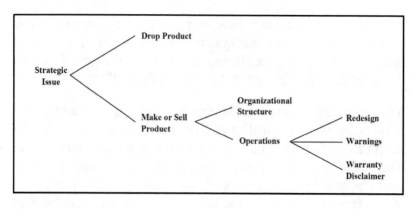

Strategic Approach

The strategic approach focuses on your fundamental business strategy and addresses this question: Should you continue to make products that subject the company to potential liability? In answering this question, you might decide to drop products on the basis of your litigation experience and the size of damage awards. But this knee-jerk decision might be an overreaction that would result in the loss of significant business opportunities.

For a deeper strategic analysis, consider the rationale for strict liability (a theory providing that companies are liable for selling a defective product even when they are not negligent). This theory is based on the assumption that companies are simply intermediaries that can raise prices to pass on product liability costs to customers. With this rationale in mind, your strategic analysis should focus on whether your company can indeed pass on its product liability costs (as the theory predicts) or whether it must bear the costs because of an inability to increase prices. In other words, the analysis should focus on who pays, rather than on whether there is liability.

To illustrate this analysis, let's assume that you work for a company in the tobacco industry, which has incurred high product liability costs over the years. Settlements and jury verdicts have pushed the product liability in this industry to hundreds of billions of dollars. Faced with this immense liability, a knee-jerk reaction might lead you to decide that your company should drop cigarettes as a product.

But a deeper analysis should focus on whether your company can pass this liability on to customers. For example, after tobacco companies agreed to a $206 billion settlement with 46 states in 1998, the companies raised their prices by 76 cents a pack. This allowed them to fund the settlement despite a 7% drop in cigarette consumption. As a *Wall Street Journal* article noted: "Where does the [state settlement] money come from? Generally speaking, not the bottom line....Viewed from the consumer perspective, the settlements effectively transfer vast wealth from smokers to states and lawyers on both sides."[12] This analysis, by the way, is not to suggest that companies should manufacture and sell cigarettes, because there are other factors besides an economic analysis that should determine that decision!

Organizational Approach

After you make the strategic decision to continue a product line, you should review your organization's structure. This review will bring into play one of the foundations of capitalism—the concept of limited liability. Under this concept, when you buy stock in a corporation, the most you can lose is your investment. If the company fails and declares bankruptcy, creditors cannot seize your—or other stockholders'—personal assets. In other words, the company is a "corporate veil" that protects you from liability.

This concept also applies when one company (a "parent") owns another company (a "subsidiary"). If the subsidiary fails, the parent is not liable for the subsidiary's debts. This creates an opportunity for a company to isolate product liability risks in a subsidiary. Your lawyers will create the subsidiary as an independent corporation. Your company, the parent, will typically own 100% of the subsidiary's stock. If, in the worst case scenario, major product liability damage awards are levied against the subsidiary, the parent company might lose its investment in the subsidiary but will not be liable beyond this investment.

Exceptions to the principle of limited liability are especially important to managers involved with company operations. For example, if the parent corporation does not treat a subsidiary as an independent corporation, courts will "pierce the corporate veil" and hold the parent liable for the subsidiary's creditors.

Several years ago, world-class race car driver Mark Donohue was killed when a tire manufactured by Goodyear blew out during a race. When his estate sued Goodyear in the United States, the company argued that because the tire was manufactured by its United Kingdom subsidiary, the lawsuit should be filed in England. But the trial judge allowed the case to proceed against the parent company on the grounds that Goodyear dominated the subsidiary rather than treating it as an independent corporation.

A comment on the case in *Forbes* observed that: "One of the reasons companies set up subsidiaries, in fact, is to use the corporate form to limit legal liability. For the same reason that you can't sue GM shareholders if a Chevrolet's brakes fail, you can't sue Goodyear if a tire made by its subsidiary has a blowout.... [But] companies get into trouble over the question of whether they have dominated subsidiaries to the extent that they are indistinguishable from the parent."[13]

Courts are also inclined to pierce the corporate veil when a subsidiary is inadequately capitalized, when the parent describes a subsidiary as a department or division (rather than as a corporation), when a subsidiary does not follow normal legal requirements such as holding regular board meetings, or when a parent uses the subsidiary's property as its own.

The general message for managers is clear. Your attorneys will be able to incorporate a subsidiary that can be used to house products that carry significant product liability risks. But to be protected by the corporate veil that your attorneys have created, you should allow the subsidiary to operate as an independent entity.

Operations Approach

After you decide to continue a product line, in addition to considering your organizational structure you should review your operations. Your operations approach to minimizing product liability costs should relate to the three types of product defects discussed previously in this chapter: design, manufacturing, and marketing. The importance of eliminating manufacturing defects is obvious and has already received considerable attention as a result of quality programs that many companies worldwide have adopted. This section will focus instead on a process companies can use to eliminate design and marketing defects, which are especially common forms of product liability. The design/marketing process has six key steps.

1. Form a product safety team. In assembling teams, you might be inclined to invite participants with engineering backgrounds who understand product design. The risk is that engineers, while bright and logical, might be too focused on the product's intended purpose and uncomfortable thinking about how "real" people (that is, non-engineers) actually use products. For reasons discussed in the next step, your product safety team should include representatives from functions throughout the company. You should also include potential customers on the team and invite them to describe how they might use your product.

2. Identify foreseeable uses. Recall that you must design a product and develop warnings based on the foreseeable ways in which customers might use your product—not just the ways you intend them to use the product. Thus, the product safety team should consider all possible ways customers might use the product. For example, I have led simulations where product safety teams composed of experienced managers brainstorm possible uses of a hairdryer. Within a matter of seconds, team members think of uses such as:

- Dry clothing
- Start barbeques
- Shrink plastic
- Dry glue and paint
- Defrost refrigerators
- Thaw frozen pipes
- Dry pets
- Remove stickers
- Dry fingernail polish
- Dust
- Defrost locks

3. Identify risks. The product safety team should next identify risks associated with all the foreseeable uses. For example, in reviewing the hairdryer's foreseeable uses, you might decide there are risks associated with using the hairdryer to dry glue and paint, but that using the hairdryer to defrost locks creates little risk of injury.

4. Redesign the product. The product safety team should then determine whether the product can be redesigned to eliminate the identified risks. In considering design issues, the team should focus generally on a risk-utility analysis and the questions noted previously, in the section on design defects.

5. Develop warnings. The team should develop warnings (and safety instructions) for the risks that cannot be eliminated through redesign. In conducting simulations with product safety teams, I have found that team members tend to skip discussing redesign (Step 4) and move directly to developing warnings once risks have been identified. This is a mistake because a court may not allow warnings as a defense if a safer design is available.

For example, a worker suffered a brain injury when a 16-inch Goodrich tire exploded as he attempted to mount it on a 16.5-inch rim. A prominent warning label attached to the tire contained the following warnings in red and yellow highlights. The worker ignored these warnings:

D A N G E R

NEVER MOUNT A 16″ SIZE DIAMETER TIRE ON A 16.5″ RIM. Mounting a 16″ tire on a 16.5″ rim can cause severe injury or death. While it is possible to pass a 16″ diameter tire over the lip or flange of a 16.5″ size diameter rim, it cannot position itself against the rim flange. If an attempt is made to seat the bead by inflating the tire, the tire bead will break with explosive force.

Failure to comply with these safety precautions can cause the bead to break and the assembly to burst with sufficient force to cause serious injury or death.

In the worker's lawsuit against Goodyear, the Supreme Court of Texas affirmed a jury award of $5.5 million in damages.[14] The court noted that "a product may be unreasonably dangerous because of a defect in manufacturing, design, or marketing." In this case, because there was evidence that the tire was designed defectively, the warning label did not excuse the design defect. As the court observed (quoting a legal authority): *"Warnings are not, however, a substitute for the provision of a reasonably safe design.*" (The court added the italics for emphasis.)

6. Review warranties. Finally, product safety teams should determine what, if any, warranties should accompany the product. Your company can avoid liability for express warranties simply by not giving them. In marketing your products, you can also attempt to disclaim express warranties, but the disclaimer will not work if it conflicts with an express warranty.

For example, a warranty from a clothing manufacturer stated that the company would provide a replacement if the product did not provide "one year of normal wear." Below this statement, in small type, was a disclaimer stating that the warranty would not apply if the garment was "worn out." If tested in court, the one-year warranty should prevail over the disclaimer.

You can also disclaim warranties that the law provides automatically —the implied warranties discussed earlier in this chapter. To disclaim the implied warranty of merchantability, the disclaimer must specifically mention the word "merchantability" and, if in writing, must be conspicuous. The implied warranty of fitness for a particular purpose can be disclaimed through a conspicuous disclaimer in writing. For examples of disclaimers, simply visit your favorite website. Chances are that you will find disclaimers similar to those found at Amazon.com (in print twice as large as other print at the website):

AMAZON.COM DISCLAIMS ALL WARRANTIES, EXPRESS OR IMPLIED, INCLUDING, BUT NOT LIMITED TO, IMPLIED WARRANTIES OF MERCHANTABILITY AND FITNESS FOR A PARTICULAR PURPOSE.

This section has examined three business approaches—strategic, organizational, and operational—that you can use to seize competitive advantage by minimizing product liability risks. You are now ready to climb to the balcony in an attempt to reframe product liability to meet the interests of both your company and its customers.

Align the Strategy Pillar with the Law Pillar by Reframing Product Liability to Create Value

With their focus on the Strategy Pillar and creating value for shareholders, business leaders tend to act defensively when faced with product liability risks. For example, as we have seen, many companies have decided to drop product lines in an attempt to avoid product liability litigation.

When running simulations involving the six-step new product process, I have discovered that managers can become agitated when discussing product liability, especially when the law enables customers to recover damages for injuries that result from using products for purposes other than those the manufacturer intended. Often, the simulations bring to mind stories managers have heard or experiences they have had with their own customers' misuse of products. Some of these stories are urban myths (or at least I cannot locate them in published case reports)—such as the one about the person whose cat exploded when he attempted to dry it in a microwave.

But other stories, often drawn from the executives' experiences and from case examples, are true, including the Goodyear case in which the worker ignored the tire warnings. Managers in my executive programs are especially critical of judges who push the boundaries of foreseeability and of customers who misuse products. These negative reactions can cloud opportunities to create value based on customer interests.

To illustrate, let's return to the hairdryer example. You might consider the list of foreseeable uses as examples of customer stupidity, because it shows that customers use hairdryers for purposes other than drying hair. But what if you changed your mindset to focus on your customers' interests? What are they trying to tell you when they use hairdryers for a variety of purposes? The common theme in the list is that customers need warm, moving air. They do not have access to products on the market that meet this need; consequently, they must use hairdryers for these purposes.

Companies that move beyond a purely legal focus in their design review (that is, beyond focusing on developing designs that minimize liability) and use information from the process to develop new products have an opportunity to meet customer interests while creating shareholder value. As legendary General Motors executive Alfred Sloan stated in a letter to shareholders:

> To discuss Consumer Research as a functional activity would give an erroneous impression. In its broad implications it is more in the nature of an Operating Philosophy, which to be fully effective, must extend through all phases of the business [and] serve the customer in ways [in] which the customer wants to be served.[15]

"All phases of the business" should include considering the Law Pillar of decision making. In other words, law should be used not only to control costs but also to generate new product ideas.

Identifying customer needs extends beyond initial development of new products. Once your product is on the market, it becomes important for you to review your customers' complaints about your product, their warranty claims, and their lawsuits against your company. This form of data mining is especially useful as you continue to redesign your products to maintain competitive advantage.

Opportunities for you to create or retain value extend to product delivery. For example, at one time Domino's Pizza guaranteed pizza delivery within thirty minutes or customers would receive a discount. After several traffic accidents involving Domino's drivers, the company faced public criticism and lawsuits.

If you were a Domino's executive, how might you handle this problem? One response might be to require continuous training of your drivers. But it is likely that training would be costly and might not significantly reduce the number of accidents. Better screening of potential drivers would probably lead to the same result. Another approach would be to drop your thirty-minute guarantee. But you might lose a significant marketing advantage and the opportunity to provide the best service to your customers.

Domino's opted for the last approach, dropping the thirty-minute guarantee. In doing so, however, rather than complaining about the negative impact the law had on its ability to serve customers, the company asked the question Alfred Sloan suggested: "What do our customers really want?" The company discovered that although customers want their pizza delivered as soon as possible, an important reason for that speedy delivery is that they want their pizza served hot. The solution? A new service-enhancing product—a bag that contains heating coils that keeps the pizza hot until delivery.

Key Takeaways

Product liability is one of the most important risks facing businesses worldwide. This risk relates especially to a key business stakeholder—your customers. Despite its negative impact on companies, product liability enables opportunities to create value. To develop these opportunities, you should:

1. **Become legally savvy about product liability.** You should understand the three basic legal theories that form product liability law and how they apply to the three product defects

that lead to liability: design defects, manufacturing defects, and marketing defects.

2.   **Manage product liability risks.** Once you decide to make or sell a product, you should decide whether to isolate liability within a subsidiary. You should also make operational decisions relating to warranty disclaimers and use the six-step design and marketing process.

3.   **Create value by using product liability to identify customer needs and interests.** For example, your foreseeable use analysis provides valuable data on your customers' needs for new products.

3 Use Employment Law to Attract and Retain the Best Business Talent

The worldwide McKinsey report mentioned in Chapter 1 concluded that employees are one of a company's four key stakeholders (along with customers, the government, and investors) who have the greatest effect on a company's economic value. In the past, an organization's assets were measured in terms of land, buildings, and equipment. In today's information-based economy, the intellectual capital your employees create might be your key asset. As such, your ability to find and retain the best employees is a critical element in creating value. Your success in this endeavor depends in large part on your understanding of employment law, which touches every aspect of a company's relationship with its employees.

As noted in Chapter 1, employment law covers many areas, including background checks, collective bargaining agreements, discipline, employee benefits, employee handbooks, health and safety, pay, and performance. To illustrate the Three Pillar model, this chapter addresses two of the most important and controversial areas: wrongful discharge and discrimination. A recent Chubb Private Company Risk Survey concluded that 45% of surveyed companies were concerned about the topics covered in this chapter: "a lawsuit for wrongful termination, sexual harassment, discrimination or retaliation."[1] And 22% of those surveyed felt that an employment lawsuit would cause significant damage to their companies. The first half of this chapter covers wrongful discharge and the second half focuses on discrimination.

Legal Briefing on Wrongful Discharge Law

As a starting point, you should be familiar with the basic legal concepts relating to wrongful discharge. The fundamental principle that governs wrongful discharge in the United States is the employment-at-will rule. Under this rule, you can hire and fire employees at will in all states but Montana (which requires good cause for dismissals). This rule does not apply to employees governed by union collective bargaining agreements, but the overwhelming majority of US employees in private industry do not belong to unions.

Most other countries do not follow the employment-at-will rule. Instead, the typical approach is that employers must provide advance notice when employees are discharged and might have to compensate employees who are fired without cause. The length of the notice varies from country to country. In Japan, for instance, thirty days' notice is required, while in India the notice period is one to three months, depending on the employer's size.[2]

In recent years, various US states have moved closer to the law in other countries as courts have developed three exceptions to the employment-at-will rule. First, in most states, the rule does not apply when companies make statements to employees or in company documents that create contractual rights that override the rule. For example, during a company's negotiations with a prospective employee (who was later hired as Director of Marketing), a company officer mentioned that "if you are doing the job, you can be assured that you will not be discharged." When the employee was later discharged, he sued the company claiming that the oral statement prevented the company from firing him without cause and that there was no cause for the dismissal. He recovered $300,000.[3]

Second, in some states a company must act in good faith when dismissing employees. In one case, a company fired a salesperson who had worked for the company for twenty-five years. In awarding damages to the salesperson, a jury decided that the termination (which occurred shortly after the salesperson had secured a $5 million order) resulted from the company's desire to reduce the employee's bonus, which would have been due as a result of the sale. An appellate court noted that the employee's contract was "a classic terminable at will employment contract… [that] reserved to the parties an explicit power to terminate the contract without cause." But the court affirmed the jury decision on the grounds that a company's decision to fire an employee must be made in good faith.[4]

Third, in most states a dismissal may not violate public policy. For example, a hospital hired a nurse as an at-will employee. She went on a camping trip with her supervisor and employees of other hospitals. During the trip, members of the group staged a parody of the song "Moon River," which allegedly featured them "mooning" the audience. The nurse refused to participate in this parody and in other activities that made her feel uncomfortable. Before the trip, the nurse had received favorable performance evaluations. Shortly after the trip, she was terminated.

When the lower courts dismissed a lawsuit filed by the nurse, she appealed to the Supreme Court of Arizona. The court held that "an employer may fire for good cause or for no cause. He may not fire for bad cause—that which violates public policy." Does refusal to participate in mooning violate public policy? The Supreme Court justices admitted that "We have little expertise in the techniques of mooning." But, citing the state's indecent exposure law, the court concluded that "termination of employment for refusal to participate in public exposure of one's buttocks is a termination contrary to the policy of this state...."[5]

In addition to these three exceptions—contractual rights, good faith, and public policy—fired employees often allege that they have been defamed in connection with the discharge. Defamation occurs when someone makes untrue statements that harm another person's reputation.

In one case, an employer fired an insurance salesperson named Larry. When he was unable to find employment with other firms, he hired an investigator. Posing as a prospective employer, the investigator contacted the office manager of the firm where Larry had worked. The office manager told the investigator that Larry was "irrational, ruthless, and disliked by office personnel... a classical sociopath... a zero, a Jekyll and Hyde person who was lacking... scruples." Because the statements were untrue, this conversation cost the employer $1.9 million in damages when Larry filed suit for defamation.[6]

Performance reviews are a fertile source of potential defamatory statements. The following statements, allegedly from actual performance evaluations, illustrate the danger.[7]

- "He's so dense, light bends around him."
- "Since my last report, the employee reached rock bottom and began to dig."
- "He would argue with a signpost."
- "If you stand close enough to him you can hear the ocean."
- "Takes an hour and a half to watch 60 Minutes."
- "If he were any more stupid he'd have to be watered twice a week."
- "His men would follow him anywhere, but only out of morbid curiosity."

The combination of the exceptions to the employment-at-will rule with the defamation claims has produced a judicial lottery in which some employees win large damage awards and many win nothing. California is notorious for large awards in wrongful discharge cases. Several years ago, when I was a visiting professor at Stanford University, an article in the local paper told the story of a Silicon Valley employee, David, who was fired by an electronics firm. According to the article, David, a top salesperson for the company, was replaced by someone who had financial ties to the manager who fired David. Company representatives investigated the matter, but then claimed that they lost their file. When David sued the company for wrongful discharge, he also claimed that the company distributed defamatory information about him. Based on this combination of factors, the jury awarded David $61 million in damages. The article indicated that the company planned an appeal.[8]

Large awards are not limited to California. A jury in Kentucky awarded two former Ashland Oil employees $70 million (more than half of the company's annual earnings) after the company wrongfully discharged them when they protested illegal foreign payments. The case was eventually settled for "only" $25 million.[9] And a Texas jury awarded a former energy company employee $124 million for wrongful discharge after the employee refused to prepare documents that contained misleading information. The Texas case was also eventually settled for $25 million.[10]

The Law Pillar: Wrongful Discharge and Defamation Risk Management

Given the high financial risks associated with wrongful discharge litigation, most companies have taken numerous measures to minimize liability. Consider in particular three approaches for preventing potential liability: (1) review your hiring practices, (2) train managers and review your documents, and (3) minimize defamation liability.

Review Your Hiring Practices

First, review your hiring practices. Careful screening of prospective employees to eliminate those who might be candidates for dismissal down the road is an obvious approach. Unfortunately, obtaining employment histories from former employers can be difficult. They are often reluctant to discuss job performance because of defamation risks.

Another hiring strategy is to hire temporary employees. Companies outside the United States have long used this strategy in countries where the costs of dismissal are high because the law provides automatic compensation when employees are discharged without cause. For example, a few years ago I helped open a University of Michigan center in Paris. Before I interviewed potential staff members, a French lawyer instructed me on the importance of hiring staff on short-term contracts. At the end of such contracts, she explained, the University could decide whether to renew or terminate the contracts without the costs that would be associated with dismissing a regular employee. In France, more than 80% of new employment contracts signed each year are for temporary employment.[11]

Training and Document Review

A second strategy for minimizing liability is directed toward statements that might create an exception to the employment-at-will rule. You should train and constantly remind managers that statements to staff such as "as long as you do well, you'll have a job" create an expectation that the company will only fire employees when there is good cause.

You should also review company documents and delete language that might overturn the employment-at-will rule. A few years ago I gave a presentation at a large utility company in Texas. In preparing the talk, I reviewed the company's recruiting brochure in the MBA Career Development Office at the Ross School of Business. A statement in the brochure caught my eye. To paraphrase, it read: "After joining the company, you will first participate in an orientation program. You then will be assigned to a permanent position that is consistent with your career goals." The problem here is "permanent"; a word that should be *permanently* avoided in all company documents. During my presentation, I quoted the brochure. Immediately afterward, two human resource managers mentioned their concern about this language and asked me for a copy of the brochure.

The following year, the company invited me back for another presentation. Once again, I visited the Ross Career Development Office to review the recruiting brochure. I noticed that the company had a new brochure. When I turned to the page with the statement quoted above, I discovered that the language had been "slightly" altered. Paraphrasing again, it now read: "At the end of the orientation program, an interesting career *may* be waiting for you" (my emphasis). Clearly, the company understood the problem with the language in the original brochure!

Minimize Defamation Liability

The third strategy is to try to reduce your company's liability for defamatory statements by instructing your staff that they should not comment on the job performance of former employees. In fact, they should make no comments at all but should, instead, direct all inquiries about a former employee to human resources. A human resources professional will then provide very limited information regarding the time of employment and title but will not discuss performance matters.

But even when communications about a former employee are

handled by human resources, a "no comment" approach can have drawbacks. One problem is the difficulty prospective employers face when trying to investigate someone's employment history. Another problem arises when you dismiss someone for reasons unrelated to performance (for example, when you downsize your business) and want to say something positive about the former employee to a prospective employer. Furthermore, as discussed in the next section, a "no comment" approach will not eliminate all types of liability. Nevertheless, all respondents in a survey of Fortune 500 firms indicated that they do not provide references.[12]

Align the Strategy Pillar with the Law Pillar by Reframing Wrongful Discharge Law to Create Value

The fear of a headline damage award like those rendered by juries in California, Texas, Kentucky, and elsewhere has caused managers to focus on the risk management approaches just described. However, these approaches have limitations that are illustrated by the "no comment" strategy.

Problems with the "No Comment" Strategy

The "no comment" approach to requests for information from prospective employers might reduce your company's liability based on conversations with outsiders, but it overlooks other types of conversation. For example, what would you say if one of your staff asks why an employee is no longer with the company? A "no comment" response is likely to cause morale problems and unrest among remaining employees.

On the other hand, if you do choose to comment, a statement that is untrue opens the door to a defamation lawsuit. For example, an employee who had worked for a company for forty-one years was fired after the company accused him of stealing a $35 company phone. The employee, who claimed that the phone belonged to him, sued the company for defamation after it posted notices on company bulletin boards accusing him of theft. A jury awarded the employee $15.6 million in damages and the case was later settled.[13]

What if you say nothing to either outsiders or insiders? Might there be defamation liability for actions alone? Yes, said an Illinois federal court—in a case involving a trader on the Chicago Board of Trade who had worked for a brokerage firm for twelve years. The broker claimed that one afternoon, three of the firm's officials unexpectedly came to his office and, in plain view of other employees, interrogated him about his expense reports. They then escorted him from the office without allowing him to speak to his staff or take his belongings. He alleged that other brokerage firms would not discharge a high-level employee in this manner unless there had been a violation of criminal law or a breach of ethics. When the firm asked the court to dismiss the case, the judge denied the request.[14]

Still another flaw with the "no comment" approach is the risk of liability for what you say to the discharged employee, even if no one else is present. For example, let's assume that you fire one of your employees, Frank, and you advise him privately that the reason for the discharge is that he is a classic sociopath, which is not true. Frank then applies for a job with another company. A manager from that company calls you and asks why Frank was fired. You refuse to comment, in accordance with company policy. The manager then asks Frank to explain why he left the company. Frank's choice is to explain honestly that you told him he is a classic sociopath, or to lie about the reasons you gave, which is not an acceptable alternative.

After hearing Frank explain the truth, the manager understandably

81

decides not to hire Frank. Frank then sues you for defamation. "Wait a minute," you say. "I did not defame Frank. He defamed himself by passing on the information." This is still defamation, according to courts in several states, because Frank had no choice. He was compelled to defame himself.

In one "compelled self-defamation" case, four insurance company employees were terminated for what the company called "gross insubordination." The company policy was to provide prospective employers with only dates of employment and the final job titles of former employees. When these employees told prospective employers the reasons they were given for the discharge, they had difficulty finding jobs. The Supreme Court of Minnesota upheld a damage award of $300,000 to the employees.[15]

In summary, the conventional "no comment" approach overlooks potential liability based on (1) conversations with internal staff, (2) actions that might be defamatory, and (3) comments made privately to an employee.

Manage by Fact

Conventional risk management strategies tend to address a symptom (potentially large damage awards) of a deeper problem that is revealed when you climb to the balcony to gain perspective: the real cost of wrongful discharge litigation. The Rand Corporation conducted an in-depth empirical study that assessed the impact of employment-at-will rule erosion following development of the exceptions discussed in the Legal Briefing that opens this chapter. The study concluded that the indirect costs of these exceptions are 100 times greater than the direct legal costs that receive the most attention from managers—that is, jury awards, settlements, and attorney fees. The indirect costs include keeping poor performers, making large severance payments, and forcing managers to use complex and time-consuming processes before discharging anyone.

The view from the balcony demonstrates that company expenditures to avoid litigation far exceed actual litigation costs.[16]

By reframing the legal concern (high litigation costs) as a business concern (the impact of keeping poor performers or giving them large severance packages), you can then reexamine your risk management solutions with an eye toward value creation. One solution that should immediately come to mind is a key feature of a quality program: manage by fact. In other words, tell the truth. This solution is especially attractive because it meets the interests of both your company and its employee stakeholders.

Two aspects of truth-telling are especially important in the context of wrongful termination. First, telling the truth about an employee's poor performance is critically important in the performance review process, because your ability to show cause for discharge reduces a poor performer's chances for a successful lawsuit under the exceptions to the employment-at-will rule. As a human resources director at a large utility company once told me, "We are an at-will company, but we always try to show cause."

Honestly though, honesty is sometimes easier said than done. It is often difficult for managers to be completely candid when they sit down with employees to review performance. For example, one company rated employees on a scale of 1 to 10, with 10 as the best rating. No supervisor at this company gave employees a rating of lower than 8, and the average score was 9.[17] In an environment where managers are not candid and honest, even poor performers might walk into court with performance reviews indicating that their work has been "great." The solution is to use candid, fact-based statements when you conduct performance reviews.

Many companies have recently decided on another approach—they have abandoned performance reviews. Cigna Corporation, for example, eliminated its performance review system in 2015. In its place, the company encourages managers to meet frequently with employees, with an emphasis on coaching them. According to the company's chief learning officer, "Employees are saying, 'This is the first real honest conversation I've had with my manager about me, about what I should do, instead of these goals that aren't really related to me.'"[18]

The second aspect of truth-telling that is important in the context of wrongful termination is that truth is a defense in a defamation action. As we have seen, the "no comment" approach that dominates business today is only partially effective because it focuses on external communications, whereas liability may extend to comments made within the company. The "no comment" approach also makes it difficult for companies to uncover information about prospective employees. In contrast, a truth-telling approach will protect a company across the board—whether the communication is with prospective employers, other employees within the firm, or the discharged employee.

Beyond its impact in wrongful termination cases, truth-telling is important in establishing trust. In a world of flat, lean organizations and new forms of business alliances, trust is essential to achieve competitive advantage. As noted in an article in *The Economist*:

> The arguments in favour of trust seem overwhelming. Trust reduces the costs and delays associated with traditional monitoring systems and formal legal contracts. It enables companies to engage the hearts and minds of their employees, not just their passive compliance.[19]

In short, replacing "no comment" policies with management by fact and truth-telling in your internal and external communication represents a major step toward creating an environment of trust.

Legal Briefing on Discrimination

We now turn to the second important and controversial employment law topic covered in this chapter—discrimination. Managers need a clear understanding of anti-discrimination law. Depending on country or local law, the following categories might be protected from employer discrimination: age, appearance, disability, marital status, national origin, pregnancy, race, receipt of welfare, religion, sex, and sexual orientation. To illustrate company approaches toward addressing discrimination concerns, this section focuses generally on sex discrimination, and specifically sexual harassment.

Sex discrimination and sexual harassment cases can result in huge damage awards. For example, in 2010, a jury awarded $250 million to several female staff members in a sex discrimination case. In 2011, an employee who alleged sexual harassment was awarded $95 million. And in 2012, a physician's assistant won $168 million in a sexual harassment lawsuit.[20] Although plaintiffs in cases such as these often receive less than the jury award as a result of caps on damages, appeals, or negotiated settlements, the financial impact on business can still be severe. Even allegations of sexual harassment can destroy a business, which happened to a public relations firm in late 2015.[21]

United States sexual harassment law is grounded in the Civil Rights Act of 1964, which makes sex discrimination illegal. While sex discrimination includes sexual harassment, the definition of sexual harassment was unclear until a landmark Supreme Court decision in 1986, *Meritor v. Vinson*. According to the Court, a key fact in determining whether conduct is lawful is whether it is welcome. Conduct that is welcomed does not constitute harassment; unwelcomed conduct is harassment. In the words of the US Equal Employment Opportunity Commission ("EEOC"), "Harassment is unwelcome conduct that is based on race, color, religion, sex (including pregnancy), national origin, age (40 or older), disability or genetic information."[22]

The Supreme Court explained that there are two types of unwelcome conduct. One type is *quid pro quo* or "this for that" sexual harassment. "This" is an economic benefit that a manager might offer someone in exchange for "that," which is a sexual relationship. The classic example is the "casting couch" scenario, where a movie director says to a young starlet "Sleep with me, and I'll make you a star."

The second type of sexual harassment results when the work environment is hostile because of sexual misconduct. In defining "hostile environment" sexual harassment, the Supreme Court quoted guidelines developed by the EEOC. These guidelines provide that "sexual misconduct constitutes prohibited 'sexual harassment,' whether or not it is directly linked to the grant or denial of an economic *quid pro quo*, where 'such conduct has the purpose or effect of unreasonably interfering with an individual's work performance or creating an intimidating, hostile, or offensive working environment.'"

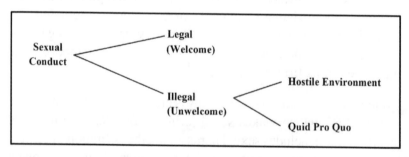

Laws in other countries now reflect the US Supreme Court's definition of sexual harassment. For example, under a 2012 French law, sexual harassment is defined as putting someone in an intimidating, hostile, or offensive situation. Penalties for violating the law are harsh and include a possible three-year prison sentence.[23] Companies have also responded to the ruling by developing internal codes of conduct. As an article in *The Economist* noted: "A Supreme

Court ruling in 1986 made firms liable if they allow a 'hostile environment' in which harassment is tolerated. This led to the near-universal adoption of codes of conduct...."[24]

The Law Pillar: Sexual Harassment Risk Management

In decisions after *Meritor*, the Supreme Court provided companies with guidelines that can minimize liability for sexual harassment. A leading case was brought by an ocean lifeguard who worked for the City of Boca Raton, Florida. She claimed that her two supervisors created a "sexually hostile atmosphere" by subjecting her and other female lifeguards to "uninvited and offensive touching." She also alleged that that they made lewd remarks and spoke of women in offensive terms. The trial court found that one of the supervisors:

> repeatedly touched the bodies of female employees without invitation, would put his arm around Faragher, with his hand on her buttocks, and once made contact with another female lifeguard in a motion of sexual stimulation. He made crudely demeaning references to women generally, and once commented disparagingly on Faragher's shape. During a job interview with a woman he hired as a lifeguard, Terry said that the female lifeguards had sex with their male counterparts and asked whether she would do the same.[25]

Based on these findings, the trial court held that Boca Raton was liable for sexual harassment. The Supreme Court upheld this decision. The Court noted that employers are liable when they take tangible action—for example, causing economic injury to an employee such as denying a promotion or raise. But even when the employer does not take action, as in this case, an employer is liable unless it can prove two elements: "(a) that the employer exercised reasonable care to prevent and correct promptly any sexually harassing behavior, and (b) that the plaintiff employee unreasonably failed to take advantage of any preventive or corrective opportunities provided by the employer."

The practical message from this language is that employers should take three measures to prevent liability. First, adopt an anti-harassment policy. Ideally, the policy will provide examples of the acts that are prohibited by the company. Here is an example of prohibited acts listed in one company's policy: "Repeated, offensive sexual flirtations, advances, propositions; continued or repeated verbal abuse of a sexual nature; graphic verbal commentaries about an individual's body; sexually degrading words used to describe an individual; display of sexually suggestive objects or pictures."[26]

Second, employers should establish a complaint procedure that will result in prompt correction of any suspect behavior. This procedure should provide alternative avenues for complaint—for example, to a supervisor, to human resources, or to a peer group. Both the anti-harassment policy and the complaint procedure should be communicated effectively to employees.

Third, employers should provide sexual harassment training. The law in California, for example, requires companies with fifty or more employees to provide supervisors with sexual harassment training.

Through training, employees should understand that actions and statements are perceived differently by men and women. For example, how would you feel about being sexually propositioned in the workplace? A study cited by a Florida court found that around two-thirds of men would be flattered, while fifteen percent would feel insulted. These proportions are reversed for women. As a result, the court decided that the test to determine whether a hostile environment exists depends on how a reasonable woman would view the workplace.[27] With this perspective in mind, the

Golden Rule (do unto others as you would have them do unto you) is not a useful guideline. A better guide is the Platinum Rule: do unto others as they would want done to themselves.

A company that takes these three measures should have a greater chance of success in defending a sexual harassment case. For example, in one case decided after the Supreme Court stated its guidelines, an employee was assigned to a new shift. One of her coworkers made comments (among others) "in front of other co-workers that if Fenton had any more children she would be wider than the Grand Canyon and that she would have to use shims off of one of the machines in the shop to make any man want her again; that he was going to call 1-900 numbers and 'play with himself', and that men 'only want one thing from you.'"

The employee reported the coworker's comments to a supervisor, who the same day met with the plant superintendent. A report was immediately made to a human resources manager, who met with the complaining employee the next day. The manager investigated the matter and within four days the coworker who made the comments was reassigned to another area. The coworker was also advised that if the comments continued he would be subject to disciplinary action. The court concluded that the employer was not liable because it took prompt corrective action.[28]

Even with these measures in place, however, plaintiffs might play a trump card called "retaliation" that can result in employer liability. It is illegal for employers to retaliate against employees who file discrimination complaints or who complain to an employer about discrimination. Retaliation encompasses actions beyond firing the employee and could come in the form of decisions relating to pay, work assignments, or training opportunities.

Retaliation claims can even be made by an associate of the person who filed a complaint. For example, a company fired an engineer three weeks after his fiancé filed a sex discrimination complaint. He then sued the company, alleging retaliation. In a 2011 decision, the US Supreme Court decided that his lawsuit could proceed to trial, noting that "We think it obvious that a reasonable worker might be dissuaded from engaging in protected activity if she knew that her fiancé would be fired."[29]

The EEOC offers several risk management guidelines companies can use to try to prevent retaliation claims, including the following:[30]

- Avoid publicly discussing the allegation
- Be mindful not to isolate the employee
- Avoid reactive behavior such as denying the employee information/equipment/benefits provided to others performing similar duties
- Do not threaten the employee, witnesses or anyone else involved in processing a complaint

Align the Strategy Pillar with the Law Pillar by Reframing Sexual Harassment Law to Create Value

Just the mention of sexual harassment often brings thoughts of litigation and large damage awards to a manager's mind. Some managers even consider sexual harassment training to be a necessary evil that pulls employees away from productive work and is forced on companies by the legal system. As the president of a high-tech company commented following a US Supreme Court sexual harassment decision, "I have to lay something out very bluntly. I have had very little use for lawyers. They cause more problems than they solve."[31]

But is sexual harassment a legal problem or a business problem? If there were no laws governing sexual misconduct, would it still make sense for businesses to follow the approaches that are currently mandated by law? When you climb to the balcony to move away from the legal fray and gain a broader perspective, a different picture might emerge. This perspective was best summarized by an executive vice president for a major power company who noted that sexual harassment "is a business issue. It doesn't have to do [only] with law or morality but about having a productive work force."[32]

Simply stated, your employees cannot be productive if they must worry about the abuse of power that sexual harassment represents. Studies on the incidence of sexual harassment reach varying conclusions depending on the country and the type of work at issue. For example, a 2014 study concluded that 90% of female restaurant workers in the United States have experienced sexual harassment.[33] More generally, an estimated 40% to 60% of women in United States-based companies have experienced harassment.[34] Outside the workplace, sexual harassment is more rampant. A 2014 study concluded that harassment caused 75% of women around the world to change their transportation.[35]

Women comprise half of the workforce worldwide. If 50% of women experience or witness sexual harassment on the job, 25% of your employees must worry about something other than doing a good job. And this figure does not include sexual harassment of men. According to the United States Equal Employment Opportunity Commission, over 16% of sexual harassment charges are filed by men.[36]

Companies that eliminate sexual harassment have the opportunity to seize competitive advantage by allowing their employees to focus on company interests while at the same time enhancing their career prospects by performing to their full potential. As one expert on sexual harassment noted, "there's quite a consistent body of literature that shows that [with sexual harassment] work performance declines, and as a result quality of performance, and attendance [also decline]. All of that ultimately has to hurt the company."[37]

From your perspective on the balcony, you can see that the real issue for your company extends beyond complying with the laws against sexual harassment to removing barriers that prevent your employees from being as productive as possible. As a result, your sexual harassment policy should not be limited to "We will not tolerate sexual harassment." Instead, the spirit of the policy should be "We will create a productive work environment that will enable our employees to achieve company and career success."

With this perspective, your horizon broadens to eliminating barriers beyond sexual harassment. As an employment law expert once put it, companies tend to "broadcast their sexual-harassment policies, but they have nothing in them about any other kind of harassment."[38] Yet it is clear that the Supreme Court guidelines apply to other types of harassment covered by the Civil Rights Act of 1964, such as race and religion.

For example, an African-American employee brought suit against Budget Rent-A-Car alleging racial discrimination. A federal court denied Budget's motion to dismiss the case, noting that the employee's claims, if proven, could result in a finding of racial harassment. The employee alleged that his supervisor treated him more harshly than other employees and used racial epithets. This is testimony from another employee:

> I was in his [the supervisor's] office one morning and he was looking out the window and pointed to the black service agents and remarked how lazy they were and how slow they worked and said that was typical of blacks.... [He] said that he wanted to get Anthony to quit because it would be difficult to fire him because he was black.[39]

The court noted that under the post-*Meritor* Supreme Court

guidelines, Budget did not prove that it distributed its harassment policy to employees or that it offered racial harassment training to its managers. Budget also did not prove that it promptly corrected complaints of racial harassment.

With a company policy that takes a broader perspective focusing on productivity, it is easier for all employees to understand that harassment is not limited to the acts of managers and other employees; the company even has a duty to prevent customers from engaging in discriminatory conduct. For example, a waitress sued the Pizza Hut franchise where she worked claiming hostile environment sexual harassment. Two "crude and rowdy" male customers had eaten at the restaurant several times and had made sexually offensive remarks to the waitress, such as "I would like to get into your pants."

One evening, when no one on the wait staff wanted to serve these customers, the shift manager ordered the waitress to serve them. One of the customers said "that she smelled good and asked what kind of cologne she was wearing." When she told the customer that it was "none of his business," he grabbed her by the hair. When she told the manager what happened, and that she did not want to wait on them, he responded: "You wait on them. You were hired to be a waitress. You waitress." When she delivered a pitcher of beer to the customers, one of them "pulled her by the hair, grabbed her breast, and put his mouth on her breast."

The waitress then told the manager that she was quitting and called her husband, who picked her up. At trial, an expert witness testified that the waitress, who had been sexually assaulted by a friend of her father when a teenager, "exhibited classic symptoms of post-traumatic stress disorder and major depression." In upholding a jury verdict for the waitress, an appellate court concluded that an employer should be held liable regardless of whether a hostile environment is created by "a co-employee or a nonemployee, since the employer ultimately controls the conditions of the work environment."[40]

In 2015, a federal court of appeals ruled that companies have a duty to follow their usual anti-discrimination policies even when there is an anonymous harasser. In that case, an African-American flight attendant alleged that United Airlines failed to take adequate measures after she reported a racist death threat.[41]

In cases involving sexual, racial, or religious harassment by employers or their customers, there is a clear violation of the law. But harassment in any form, whether legal or not, is harmful to employees (and their companies) because it prevents them from focusing on their work. This is the way Dow Chemical puts it when describing its policy toward lesbian, gay, bisexual, and transgender ("LGBT") workers:

> While many states in the US and abroad have yet to pass laws protecting LGBT people from being fired based on their sexual orientation or gender identity, Dow's global Respect and Responsibility policy provides the Company's employees with this protection and helps create an environment in which all employees can focus on their jobs rather than fear of being discriminated [against] for who they are.[42]

Beyond eliminating discrimination, companies that move women and minorities to leadership positions have the opportunity to create value in the form of a "diversity dividend." According to a 2015 McKinsey study of public companies in Europe and the Americas, there is a "statistically significant relationship between companies with women and minorities in their upper ranks and better financial performance."[43]

Key Takeaways

Employees are especially important stakeholders in your company. Your efforts to attract and retain the best talent depend on a solid understanding of employment law. This chapter shows how your company can create value even when addressing two of the most controversial areas of employment law—wrongful discharge and discrimination. Creating value requires that you should:

1. **Become legally savvy about employment law.** Understand the fundamental differences between the United States-based approach to firing employees (the employment-at-will rule and its exceptions) and the approach used elsewhere. And, understand that sexual harassment liability extends beyond *quid pro quo* to hostile environment claims.

2. **Manage employment law risks.** Managing wrongful discharge risk requires a review of hiring practices and company documents. To manage sexual harassment risk, develop anti-harassment policies, along with procedures to enforce those policies, and provide company training.

3. **Create value by using employment law to meet employee interests, while also benefitting your company.** Managing by fact, as it relates to wrongful discharge, has the potential to improve the quality of your talent while also building employee trust in your company. Addressing harassment as a business problem and not just a legal problem creates an environment in which employees can focus on their work—which benefits them *and* your company.

4 Use Government Regulation to Develop New Business Models

According to the McKinsey survey mentioned in Chapter 1, executives across the globe conclude that government regulators are second only to customers among the key stakeholders who have the greatest effect on a company's economic value. Another McKinsey study provides details showing why executives might reach that conclusion. According to the study, the business value from government intervention is around 30% of a company's earnings.[1]

The importance of understanding government extends to all business decision makers. In a coauthored article, CEO of BP John Browne and McKinsey expert Robin Nuttall wrote that, "The logic [of understanding government] is simple and compelling. The success of a business depends on its relationships with the external world—regulators,... activists, and legislators. Decisions made at all levels of the business, from the boardroom to the shop floor, affect that relationship."[2]

Despite this obvious logic, evidence exists that companies are failing in their attempts to work successfully with government. A global survey cited by Browne and Nuttall concluded that more than 80% of companies do not experience frequent success with regulatory decisions and attempts to influence government policy. Thus, companies that *are* able to work successfully with government have an opportunity to achieve sustainable competitive advantage.

This chapter opens with a legal briefing on government regulation. The focus then turns to the Law Pillar and managing regulatory risk, with emphasis on how companies can shape the law and use government regulation as a source of competitive advantage. The chapter closes by examining the overlap between the Strategy Pillar and Law Pillar and how, in some cases, the law can become the foundation for new directions in strategy.

Legal Briefing on Government Regulation

In countries around the world that adhere to the rule of law, government provides three key functions. First, a legislative body has primary responsibility for creating law in the form of legislation. Second, a judicial function is tasked with interpreting the law. Third, an executive function enforces the law.

In the United States, these three functions constitute the branches of government, and each branch has its own separate powers. Several countries follow this "separation of powers" approach to government, whereas in other countries the powers are intertwined. And even in the United States, the boundaries between the branches are permeable. For example, courts in the United States (a common law system) make law when they establish precedents that future courts follow.

One exception to the separation of powers model is especially relevant to business. Because it is difficult for legislatures to enact detailed legislation, they delegate the task of filling in the details to government agencies. This is necessary even when the legislation is already quite detailed. For example, Congress enacted the Dodd-Frank Act in response to the financial crisis that began in 2007. Although this 2,300-page law went into effect in 2010, this was not the end of the law-making story, because the law required government agencies to adopt 398 regulations relating to the Act.[3]

Called the "fourth branch" of the US government, these agencies have become a key interface between business and government. Professor Jonathan Turley of George Washington University noted that as a result of administrative regulations, "The shift of authority [from the other three branches] has been staggering. The fourth branch now has a larger practical impact on the lives of citizens than all the other branches combined." To back up this statement, he observed that "Today, we have 2,840,000 federal workers in 15 departments, 69 agencies and 383 nonmilitary sub-agencies.... One study found that in 2007, Congress enacted 138 public laws, while federal agencies finalized 2,926 rules, including 61 major regulations."[4]

Government agencies are especially powerful and important to business because they combine the power of all three branches of government. They make law in the form of regulations, but they also enforce the law. For example, the Federal Trade Commission ("FTC") filed a complaint against Twitter alleging that Twitter deceived consumers by failing to protect private information. As evidence, the FTC alleged that despite Twitter's policy that it had adopted measures to protect users' information, hackers were able to send out false tweets from President Obama's account to more than 150,000 people offering them an opportunity to win free gasoline. In settling with the FTC in 2010, Twitter agreed to improve security and to remain on probation for twenty years.[5]

In addition to government agency enforcement of the law, judges linked to the agencies determine whether the law has been violated. As Professor Turley noted, "As the number of federal regulations increased, however, Congress decided to relieve the judiciary of most regulatory cases and create administrative courts tied to individual agencies. The result is that a citizen is 10 times more likely to be tried by an agency than by an actual court. In a given year, federal judges conduct roughly 95,000 adjudicatory proceedings, including trials, while federal agencies complete more than 939,000."[6]

In other words, the separation of powers principle does not apply to government agencies, which make and enforce regulations and often determine, through administrative courts, whether you have violated their rules. As a result, as we will see in the next section, your interaction with these agencies in attempting to manage regulatory risk is an important aspect of legal risk management.

The Law Pillar: Government Regulation Risk Management

Two fundamental strategies can help you manage risks relating to government regulation. One strategy is to attempt to shape laws and regulation. The second strategy is for you to take action after laws and regulations become effective. Managing political risks beyond the border of your own country raises special concerns that are addressed at the conclusion of this section.

Shaping Laws and Regulations

Successful companies recognize that public policy is an important element in their success. JPMorgan Chase officially operates six lines of business.[7] But CEO Jamie Dimon called government regulation a "seventh line of business" that is important to the success of the other six lines.[8] And General Electric ("GE") puts it this way: "The success of GE depends significantly on sound public policies.... Governments, through advancing their legitimate regulatory and political interests, affect the environment in which GE operates."[9]

We now turn to five general strategies companies can use to shape legislation, as well as a specific strategy, called the public comment process, that is useful when companies are concerned about regulations that agencies propose.

Corporate Political Strategies. In their article "Corporate Political Strategy and Legislative Decision Making," Gerald Keim and Carl Zeithaml identified five key strategies that are used by companies that are politically active.[10]

1. *Constituency building.* Immediately after being elected to public office, one question dominates the thinking of a member of the legislature: Will I be reelected? As a result, legislators are especially concerned about meeting the needs of their constituents—the voters. Your efforts to influence the legislative process should involve these constituents.

   For example, let's assume that proposed legislation will affect your manufacturing facilities located in three states. You should use a three-step process to build constituent support:

   a. Identify constituents who have an interest in your company. Obvious candidates are shareholders, employees, customers, suppliers, and leaders in the community where your plants are located.
   b. Organize and educate the constituents.
   c. Develop an action plan that includes constituent contact with their elected representatives to share opinions about legislative proposals. The contact might take the form of email, letters, phone calls, and office visits.

2. *Campaign contributions.* Running for elected office is an expensive undertaking. In 2014, the winner in the Kentucky Senate race, Republican Mitch McConnell, spent more than $30 million, whereas the loser, Democrat Alison Grimes, spent more than $18 million.[11] To fund their campaigns, elected representatives spend considerable time engaged in fundraising. This has led to what is called the "Tuesday–

Thursday Club," referring to Congressional representatives who work in Washington only on Tuesday through Thursday of each week and spend the rest of the week fundraising at home.

In the United States, organizations called Political Action Committees ("PACs") are often used to raise money to support or defeat candidates for office. PACs can represent businesses (Microsoft PAC), labor (Teamsters PAC), or other interests (National Rifle Association PAC).[12] In the 2014 election cycle, the top PAC contributor was the National Association of Realtors, which contributed $3.8 million (48% to Democrats and 52% to Republicans). Foreign companies can also use the PAC structure when their American subsidiaries form PACs funded by employees in the United States. In the 2014 election cycle, the leading foreign-connected PAC contributor was UBS Americas, with total contributions of $679,000 to Democrats and $811,250 to Republicans.[13]

3. *Advocacy advertising.* Companies can use advertising as a means to reach a broad audience in an attempt to influence legislators. Unlike usual corporate advertising, which promotes a service or a product, advocacy advertising focuses on public policy concerns. For example, in the 1970s, Mobil Oil Company started an advocacy campaign regarding the need for offshore oil drilling to address the energy crisis.[14]

4. *Lobbying.* Lobbying is generally defined as an attempt to influence the decisions of government officials. Company leaders can directly engage in lobbying or they can hire professionals.

Spending on lobbying in the United States has grown

considerably over the years, from $1.57 billion in 2000 to $3.2 billion in 2015. In 2015, the top spenders were the US Chamber of Commerce ($84.7 million), the National Association of Realtors ($37.8 million), and the American Medical Association ($28.6 million). The leading issues (as measured by client reports) were the federal budget, health issues, and taxes.[15]

Growth in lobbying expenditures can parallel the success of a company. For example, in 2004, Google's lobbying expenditures totaled $180,000. By 2014, the expenditure had grown to $16.8 million.[16] During that year, Google opened its new Capitol Hill office that is roughly the size of the White House. Why? According to an article in *The Washington Post*, "Google's increasingly muscular Washington presence matches its expanded needs and ambitions as it has fended off a series of executive- and legislative-branch threats to regulate its activities and well-funded challenges by its corporate rivals."[17]

Lobbying is often seen as a self-serving activity that large companies use to increase their wealth. But this constitutionally protected activity (falling within the Constitution's 1st Amendment rights to free speech and to petition government) can also provide a useful service to government officials by giving them information they need to make informed decisions. A lobbyist who does not provide this information in a balanced manner will quickly lose credibility. As a government official in Asia put it, "Bad lobbying is telling me something I know. Average lobbying is telling me something I did not know. Excellent lobbying is telling me something I did not know and that's useful to me."[18]

Lobbying is an effective process for all organizations, not

just businesses. And responsible business leaders frequently lobby for changes in public policy that benefit society at large. According to one of the most powerful leaders in corporate America, David E. A. Carson (former CEO of the largest bank in Connecticut):

> In my career I've been involved in everything from neighborhood block watches to talking to the chief of staff of the President of the United Sates.... And everyone in between—state legislators, regulators, elected officials and bureaucrats—who can make the changes I thought would be good for our society. I've never lobbied to make more money. I've lobbied because I think the system works better if constraints are reasonable and understood.[19]

Public service in the form of lobbying beyond corporate interests is not without reward. As Carson puts it, "The people who end up with power in our society are those who get involved."

5. *Coalition building.* Coalition building is a useful tactic when you can find other businesses that share your interests. For example, Facebook's Mark Zuckerberg formed a group that was interested in education and immigration policy and Facebook also formed a trade association with Amazon, Google, and Yahoo "to make sure policymakers do nothing to hamstring the free flow of information or overly regulate technology firms."[20] Coalitions are especially useful when members of the coalition are constituents of a legislator whom you are attempting to influence (see #1 above).

Public Comment Process. We now turn to a strategy that relates specifically to proposed administrative regulations. As mentioned, government agencies adopt rules that complement legislation

Congress has adopted. This typically involves a four-step process. First, the agency does background research and drafts a proposed rule. Second, the proposed rule is published in the *Federal Register*, an official government publication. Third, the public can comment on the proposed rule. Fourth, the agency takes action on the rule in light of the comments.

Obviously, the third step is the most important to businesses because it gives them a chance to voice opinions about proposed rules. The process of submitting comments has become much easier in recent years as a result of an eRulemaking initiative. By going to a website (specifically, http://www.regulations.gov), you can easily search for rules, comments, and other documents. For example, when I tried the random search term "tennis," I discovered that the Department of Energy has proposed a requirement that anyone importing into the United States a covered product subject to an energy conservation standard must provide a certificate of admissibility. Table tennis was one of the products specifically mentioned. The comment period for this proposed rule was set at forty-five days.

Once you identify a proposed regulation that interests you, you can immediately participate in the rulemaking process by submitting a comment. Try it out. As the website suggests, "Make a difference. Submit your comments and let your voice be heard." Here is a slightly-edited example submitted by someone from Microsoft who is discussing a proposed rule on "Improving and Expanding Training Opportunities for F-1 Nonimmigrant Students with STEM Degrees....":

> Improving and expanding OPT [Optional Practical Training] for STEM students is obviously good for the US people and the US economy.

> 1. In my city (Seattle), one foreign worker creates nine

local jobs in service sector including restaurants, Medicare, transportation, education, sales, retail, etc. Foreign students under OPT are usually single and young, so they often contribute more than average foreign workers.

2. In the STEM area, it is a well-known fact that there [are not] enough US graduates to fill job positions. I have never seen or heard of a US citizen who successfully earned a degree [who] is not able to find a better position in the job market than average foreigners....

3. Diversity and foreign talent of US offices have been the cutting-edge for US businesses. All nations have talents, but only the US has the advantage of importing a large number of foreign workers. Von Neumann, Cate Blanchett, Brin Sergey, Jerry Yang were all foreign born. Marquis de Lafayette was foreign born.

As a variation on the standard comment process, regulators have developed regulatory negotiation (also called "reg-neg"). Under this variation, regulators meet with private parties in an attempt to find shared interests and to reach consensus *before* a rule is even proposed. For example, the US Environmental Protection Agency ("EPA") used the negotiated rulemaking process to establish a rule relating to emission standards for ovens that process coal into coke. The EPA first created a committee consisting of representatives of the EPA, environmental groups, the coke and steel industry, states, and unions. The committee met every two to three weeks for four months, and drafted a proposed rule that the EPA adopted fourteen months later.[21]

Post-Adoption Strategies

After a law has been adopted, there are two fundamental risk management approaches companies should consider: (1) embrace the law with vigorous compliance efforts and (2) use the court system to challenge the new law. While these two strategies might seem contradictory, the approaches can be used simultaneously to manage regulatory risk.

Embrace the law through compliance initiatives. When your lobbying and other efforts fail, there is a tendency to implement the new regulatory burdens with hostility, or at least begrudging acceptance. After all, these burdens bring with them costs that will directly affect your company's bottom line. For example, after the Dodd-Frank law became effective in 2010, banks took the following actions:[22]

- Goldman Sachs reduced its balance sheet by $56 billion in one quarter in order to, in the words of the Chief Financial Officer, "proactively comply with regulatory developments";
- Morgan Stanley reduced its assets by one-third;
- Citicorp sold more than sixty businesses and cut almost $700 billion in assets; and
- Bank of America eliminated more than $70 billion in assets, including parts of its credit card and mortgage businesses.

Banks coupled this loss in assets with a hiring binge that was necessary to comply with the new law and with accompanying regulations. JPMorgan Chase, for example, expected to add 13,000 employees, bringing its total regulatory and compliance staff to 30,000.

Despite these regulatory burdens, regulation can bring opportunities for competitive advantage. For example, while most companies had a negative reaction to the reporting requirements imposed by the Sarbanes-Oxley Act of 2002, a few firms recognized competitive advantage opportunities and used the law "as a leveraging tool to consolidate financial processes, eliminate redundant IT systems, broaden responsibility for financial controls, and integrate distant business units. Firms achieved significant cost savings, increased data integrity, and gained a more effective understanding of their own operations."[23]

These competitive advantage opportunities are available worldwide. For instance, in its response to the financial crisis, the European Union established a new regulatory framework that places significant burdens on investment firms. However, despite a "tough regulatory landscape" that is fully effective in 2017, companies that adapt to the regulations have the opportunity to "gain competitive advantage by expanding core competencies, winding down unprofitable portfolios and improving client services, and leveraging implementation synergies driven by regulations such as Dodd-Frank...."[24] These regulations provide a stimulus to strengthen internal controls and reduce risks that are under the surveillance of regulatory authorities.

In some situations, business leaders attempt to shape the law with an eye toward the competitive advantage their efforts will bring following the law's adoption. For example, a senior executive for a multinational corporation once told me that he traveled, with a group of executives who held similar positons at other global firms, to several less-developed countries. The purpose of the trip was to convince government officials to adopt and enforce stricter environmental laws.

Company efforts to push for stricter regulation might seem counterintuitive, but there is a compelling logic that drives the push for higher standards. In the wake of increasing uniformity of environmental regulations worldwide, global companies often adopt environmental standards that apply even in countries where environmental regulation is weak. These high standards result in additional costs that make it difficult for global companies to compete with local firms. Strengthening local environmental law levels the playing field by forcing local companies to incur environmental expenses similar to those of the multinationals.[25]

Challenge the law (and competitors). The second post-adoption strategy is to challenge new laws or regulations in court. Courts can even come into play before an agency ultimately adopts a regulation. In a legendary case, companies that produced peanut butter challenged a proposed government regulation specifying that peanut butter had to contain at least 95% peanut content. When this regulation was first proposed, some manufacturers were producing peanut butter that contained 20% to 25% hydrogenated oils (lard). The manufacturers fought the proposed rule because the higher peanut content would increase their costs. Through a combination of tactics that included public hearings and appeals in the court system, the regulation was delayed for twelve years. In the meantime, the rule's peanut content requirement was lowered to 90%.[26]

An electronic cigarette case provides an example of a court battle after a regulation is enacted. A company that imports and sells electronic cigarettes challenged a regulation the US Food and Drug Administration ("FDA") adopted under a federal drug law. The FDA had decided to use the regulation to prevent the importation of the plaintiff's electronic cigarettes into the United States. The case reached a federal appellate court in 2010. The court described electronic cigarettes as follows:

> Battery powered products that allow users to inhale nicotine vapor with fire, smoke, ash, or carbon monoxide. Designed to look like a traditional cigarette, each e-cigarette consists of three parts: the nicotine cartridge, the atomizer or heating element, and the battery and electronics.... The atomizer vaporizes the liquid nicotine, and the battery and electronics

power the atomizer and monitor air flow. When the user inhales, the electronics detect the air flow and activate the atomizer; the liquid nicotine is vaporized, and the user inhales the vapor.

With this definition in mind, the court decided that the FDA did not have authority to regulate electronic cigarettes as drugs and could regulate them only under less-restrictive tobacco laws.[27]

Courts, by the way, can become company allies in other ways. For example, companies can use the law and litigation as sources of competitive advantage by challenging the business practices of their competitors in court. Marketing decisions are often described in terms of the classic four "Ps": price, product, promotion, and place. The use of litigation adds a fifth "P" to the marketing mix: plaintiff.

Here is an example. For several years Apple and Samsung have engaged in a so-called "patent war" in courts around the world. In 2014, they agreed to end litigation outside the United States, but the battle continues in US courts. For instance, in 2012, a jury awarded Apple more than $1 billion on the grounds that Samsung violated Apple's patents when designing smartphones. However, that decision was appealed, and the litigation is still in process.[28] In the words of Santa Clara School of Law professor Brian Love, Samsung should emphasize to the jury that Apple "is losing marketplace share [to Samsung] and so wants to compete in the courtroom instead."[29]

Managing Political Risks that Arise Beyond Borders

The risk management strategies described thus far in this section can be effective in countries that adhere to the rule of law. But what if you decide to do business in countries where checks and balances among the branches of government are ineffective, and you are subject to the random decisions of whoever is in power? This situation calls for a political risk management strategy. As Stanford Business School professor Ken Shotts described (using as an example the risk that a government will seize your business assets)[30] there are two elements to this strategy.

First, you should determine the likelihood that the government will expropriate your assets. This depends on three key questions:

1. Does the government receive significant tax revenue from your company? If not, the chance of expropriation is higher.

2. Can the government operate your business without your expertise? If so, the chance of asset seizure is higher.

3. Will government leaders benefit politically from the expropriation? If so, the likelihood of it happening is higher.

Second, in situations where you do face the risk of expropriation, you should factor this risk into your strategic planning and implementation. For instance, you should consider measures to reduce the risk by gaining local support. These actions might include hiring local workers, offering training programs, building roads and making other infrastructure improvements, and using local sources for your production.

Aligning the Strategy Pillar with the Law Pillar to Create Value

Opportunities to create value by aligning the Strategy Pillar with the Law Pillar fall within two categories: anticipating regulation (called the "Regulatory Frontier" strategy) and ignoring regulation (called the "Regulatory Gap" strategy). Both categories bring together the Strategy Pillar and Law Pillar by focusing on stakeholder needs.

Anticipating Regulation—the Regulatory Frontier Strategy

An article in the *McKinsey Quarterly* on societal expectations of business distinguishes between issues already addressed by formal laws and regulations and issues that are "frontier expectations." The latter category includes issues such as obesity that could over time result in regulation. This is the way the authors put it:

> It had always been widely believed that the responsibility for avoiding [obesity] lay with individuals, who choose what they eat, not with the companies that make or sell fattening products. But the blame is shifting, much as the debate around tobacco shifted the responsibility from individuals to an industry perceived to be aggressively marketing addictive products. Food companies may not be forced to modify the fat and sugar content of their products, but the momentum on this issue could already be so great that lawmakers or regulators will step in and formalize social expectations by imposing new legal restraints.[31]

Companies that develop frontier thinking achieve two forms of competitive advantage. First, they are ahead of their competitors when regulations are eventually adopted. A company's approach to a frontier issue might even become a model for future regulation. Second, they might achieve a first-mover advantage by developing products and services that meet the consumer needs reflected by the social concern. In achieving this competitive advantage these companies might be able to embed their corporate social responsibilities into their strategic planning initiatives.

For example, how would you react to the possibility that the FDA would adopt a regulation that requires your company to add labels to its products showing the amount of trans fats in them? PepsiCo's Frito Lay division reacted by deciding to stop using trans fats in potato chips and other products. This turned into a marketing advantage when the company obtained FDA approval to place prominent labels on these products showing that they had no trans fats.[32]

Operating on the Regulatory Frontier can produce significant cost savings for companies. For example, Siemens decided to help its customers reduce their carbon impact by developing new green products. The result: additional revenues of €32.3 billion while preventing 377 million metric tons of carbon emissions.[33]

Beyond these savings are the benefits to society that result from a focus on stakeholder interests. For example, look what happened when Johnson & Johnson decided to invest in wellness programs for its employees. The company benefited by having a more productive workforce, coupled with healthcare savings of $250 million over a six-year period.[34] These benefits undoubtedly cascade down to employees and society at large in the form of better health and lower healthcare costs.

Ignoring Regulation—the Regulatory Gap Strategy

The goal of the Regulatory Gap strategy is to uncover gaps in existing regulations that enable you to serve customers in new ways. This strategy can lead to a complete overlap of the Strategy Pillar and Law Pillar when new business models are created based on the gaps you identify. For example, in 1967 Texas entrepreneur Rollin King and his lawyer Herb Kelleher incorporated an airline in Texas that they called Air Southwest. Their business model was based on the idea that by limiting their flights to Texas, they could escape federal regulation and charge cheaper fares. Competitors such as Continental Airlines sued them (the 5th "P" strategy described earlier), but Air Southwest prevailed and changed its name to Southwest Airlines.[35] Subsequent airline deregulation enabled the company to expand its operations beyond Texas.

Opportunities to use the Regulatory Gap strategy abound today with the sharing opportunities that technology creates. The so-called "sharing economy" includes business models that give consumers more control over their transactions such as ride sharing, room sharing, office sharing, meal sharing, clothes sharing, and solar energy sharing.[36] Jack Wroldsen, a professor of legal studies at Oklahoma State University's Spears School of Business, has observed that the disruptive innovation that accompanies these business models has changed the role of attorneys from transaction cost engineers to business disruption framers.[37] This new role requires business leaders and their lawyers to work together closely in developing strategic plans for new business models, just as King and Kelleher did when they formed Southwest Airlines.

Uber has become the poster child for the Regulatory Gap strategy. Uber's business model is based on the company's belief that taxi regulations do not cover transportation service companies that, instead of operating a fleet of cabs and hiring drivers, merely connect passengers to drivers. Uber's strategy is first to enter markets without permission from regulators and then to gather support from drivers and customers who use the service.

By 2015, five years after its launch, there were projections that Uber's value was higher than General Motors, Ford, and Honda—companies whose traditional business model Uber is disrupting.[38] With its growth, Uber has supplemented the Regulatory Gap strategy with the traditional strategies discussed previously in this chapter. For example, the company is actively lobbying for changes in the law that will clarify its ability to offer its services. In some cities, the company is also attempting to comply with local regulations. In New Delhi, India, for example, Uber has filed an application to operate a taxi company.[39]

Key Takeaways

This chapter focuses on a key stakeholder in every business—government. To manage business risks and develop opportunities arising from your interaction with government, you should:

1. **Become legally savvy about government regulation.** You should understand the three key functions of government and the important role played by administrative agencies—the "4th branch" of government. By exercising legislative, executive, and judicial functions, administrative agencies play an important role in your business success.

2. **Manage risks resulting from government regulation.** Risk management requires that you attempt to shape the laws and regulations that affect your business. This involves using several corporate political strategies, such as constituency building, lobbying, and coalition building. You can also shape the law through the public comment process that administrative agencies use. After laws have been adopted, your risk management strategy should emphasize rigorous compliance and mounting challenges to rules and regulations that are harmful to your business.

3. **Create value by meeting stakeholder needs through business strategies based on government regulation.** One key strategy, the Regulatory Frontier strategy, enables you to achieve competitive advantage by anticipating future regulations. With the other key strategy, the Regulatory Gap strategy, you should attempt to identify gaps in government regulation that enable you to serve customers in new ways.

5 Use Your Intellectual Property to Create Shareholder Value*

Take a moment to examine your surroundings. Whether you are at your kitchen table at home, sitting at an office desk, or traveling by train into the countryside, your environment is saturated with intellectual property. Intangible assets are represented on the cereal box from breakfast, in the fabric design of your desk chair, and in the whistle of the train as you pull into the next station. Even when you are hiking in the remotest place in the world, intellectual property will accompany you on your journey—possibly in the form of a backpack design, your boots, a hand-held GPS, or a simple printed map. You will find these embodiments of innovation not only in every place, but also in

* This chapter was authored by Dr. Christine Ladwig, a professor at the Harrison College of Business, Southeast Missouri State University. Professor Ladwig has many years of experience in business and law, including organizing and contributing to the management of over a half dozen biomedical businesses. She has also served as a consultant for The National Geographic Society, and other national and state organizations. Dr. Ladwig completed her graduate studies at The George Washington University (Ph.D. in biology), Southern Illinois University (joint J.D.–MAcc degree), Albany Law School (LL.M. in Intellectual Property), American University (M.A. in biology) and SUNY-Plattsburgh (M.S. in natural science/chemistry). In 2015, she was selected by the Academy of Legal Studies in Business as a finalist for the prestigious Charles M. Hewitt Master Teacher Award in honor of her teaching in the field of intellectual property.

every period of time throughout the history of the world.

In *Driving Innovation* (2008), author Michael Gollin calls intellectual property ("IP") the "invisible infrastructure of innovation" that supports us by providing comfort, convenience, and enjoyment in our everyday lives. Intellectual property has tremendous financial value—worth trillions of dollars. According to the World Intellectual Property Organization ("WIPO"), global businesses, universities, research institutions, and individuals are adding to that value at an unprecedented rate.[1] This intense escalation in innovation spurs wise IP holders to protect their inventions and creations and to strategize on the best use of these assets. A properly designed strategic IP management plan will often result in increased profits, reduced liabilities, and a company's secure and successful future for investors.

To build a legal strategy for commercial intellectual property, businesses must first understand that their intangible assets—whether as simple as a candy wrapper or as complex as a cellular phone—are part of a global framework. Awareness of the interdependence of world markets is an integral part of understanding how to develop, protect, and grow the value of intellectual property assets. Intellectual property protection laws and enforcement can vary widely from country to country; therefore, it is important to be familiar with the international legal landscape. Through that global perspective, an effective strategic company plan identifies potential IP assets and selects proper protection, all within the context of mapping organizational goals and resources.

This chapter defines and examines the nature of intellectual property and the legal forms available to protect these intangible assets. The chapter also covers strategic tools to manage IP efficiently and effectively, with a special focus on how businesses can use intangible assets to create value, which is essential for attracting investors.

Legal Briefing on Intellectual Property

Most everyone recognizes famous inventions such as Samsung's Galaxy phones or Apple's iPads as intellectual property. But few people realize how much more of the world is comprised of intangible assets. Take the "Happy Birthday to You" song, which has been sung around candle-lit birthday cakes since the 19th century. The simple "Happy Birthday" eight-note melody and lyrics have been protected by US copyright laws since 1893 and have earned their copyright holder, Warner Music Group, an estimated $2 million per year in licensing fees. "Happy Birthday" is joined internationally by millions of existing musical creations and compositions that may be classified as intellectual property.[2]

The WIPO defines intellectual property as "creations of the mind, such as inventions; literary and artistic works; designs; and symbols, names and images used in commerce."[3] We are immersed in a sea of intellectual creativity intended to improve the quality of our lives. From the cultivation of rice developed by the Chinese as early as 7,000 B.C.[4] to the forerunner of modern computers invented by British mathematician Charles Babbage in the mid-1800s,[5] individuals have been thinking about, creating, and expressing the "invisible infrastructure of innovation" for thousands of years.

For nearly as long as people have expressed their thoughts and visions, there have been rules and laws to protect the innovator and innovation alike. The various forms of intellectual property—trade secrets, trademarks, patents, and copyrights—provide differing rights and responsibilities, as well as distinctive laws governing their use and availability.

Some of the laws protecting IP are native to a particular country, such as the US Uniform Trade Secrets Act, which has been adopted in some form by almost all American states. Other laws are international, such as the World Trade Organization's Agreement on

Trade-Related Aspects of Intellectual Property Rights ("TRIPS"), which requires each member country to establish specific IP protection and enforcement procedures. Effective intellectual property statutes and rules are designed to provide IP owners with some benefit from their creative efforts, while concurrently encouraging continued innovation.

It is said that 9/10ths of an iceberg is hidden below the surface of the sea; therefore, the majority of its nature is largely unknown. The same can be said of intellectual property, where business managers must understand the entire potential IP landscape for their company. Identifying intellectual property assets, classifying them, and understanding the laws that protect these assets are among the key steps in creating and maximizing IP value. Once the "iceberg" is unveiled, a strategic plan to use and integrate IP assets fully can be set in motion.

A company's wealth is based on its assets, which may be defined as the resources the company owns that have value or expected value. The primary accounting categories of assets include working capital, fixed assets, and intangible assets. Several decades ago, an estimated seventy-five percent of a company's holdings were fixed assets, such as buildings, machinery, equipment and computers. Today, business portfolios hold, on average, 70% intangible assets, including goodwill and intellectual property.[6] Due to this tremendous shift in what constitutes the value of a company, it is increasingly important for business owners and managers to understand intellectual property assets and their associated rights.

Although international IP rights and laws vary, there are common features as well. The following sections summarize the various categories of IP rights—trade secrets, patents, trademarks, and copyrights—and also include specific examples from different countries.

Trade Secrets

A trade secret is a formula, practice, process, design, instrument, pattern, or compilation of information that has independent economic value in being not generally known or reasonably ascertainable (that is, the secret gives the owner some actual or potential competitive advantage).[7] A trade secret is fairly easy to create: identify undisclosed information that has some actual or potential value and then take reasonable means to protect its secrecy. Some examples of intangible assets protected by trade secrets include recipes, customer lists, marketing strategies, and manufacturing techniques.

The greatest advantage of a trade secret is that it may potentially remain a secret forever. In most countries, to have the protection of trade secret laws a company must take certain steps to ensure the security of the secret. These steps include physical and computer security measures, and confidentiality and nondisclosure agreements. Confidentiality agreements are especially important in licensing, where one company may be processing and manufacturing another company's trade secret products. Once a trade secret is exposed to the world and becomes part of the public domain, trade secret protection ends.

Perhaps the most famous trade secret in the world is the soft drink formula for *Coca-Cola*®, which has been continuously protected since around 1880. In addition to its global fame, *Coca-Cola*® might be the most valuable product known to mankind, generating more than $11 billion in sales annually. The Coca-Cola Company takes several precautions to protect this profitable intellectual property, including keeping the formula in a locked bank vault that can only be opened by resolution of the company's board of directors. In addition, it has been reported that only two living Coca-Cola executives know the formula at the same time, and these individuals are not allowed to travel together. In the 1970s, when a food safety government official in India requested the ingredient list for *Coca-Cola*®, the company refused and stopped exporting the product to India. Other examples of trade secrets in the United States include the Kentucky Fried Chicken recipe (which, like *Coca-Cola*®, only two living executives know at any given time), the *Farmer's Almanac*® weather-predicting formula, and the methodology used to select books for *The New York Times*® Best-Seller List.[8]

Trade secrets in the United States are protected in nearly every state by the Uniform Trade Secrets Act ("UTSA"). At the core of the UTSA legislation is an understanding of the commercial value and competitive advantage inherent in trade secrets. The UTSA provides several remedies for the misappropriation of trade secrets, including injunctions (which prevent further use of the trade secret), financial compensation, and sometimes even punitive damages (intended to punish the wrongdoer and deter others) and/or attorney fees.

As noted at the US Library of Congress website,[9] other countries also recognize and protect the rights in a trade secret. In Brazil, a violation of trade secret law is considered a crime of unfair competition, and the violator must make reparations to fix the damage caused to the intellectual property owner. Labor law in Brazil also allows employers to terminate employees for trade secret violations.

In India, unlike the United States, there are no specific trade secret laws. However, undisclosed information and secrets can be protected through breach of contract or breach of confidence actions. If there is a confidentiality agreement between two parties, for example, and one party discloses information that violates the contract, the other side is entitled to a remedy similar to those available in the United States: injunctions, monetary compensation, and return of the confidential information.[10]

China, like India, also does not have a unified trade secrets law. Numerous Chinese laws, however, provide trade secret protection, such as the Anti-Unfair Competition Law. This statute defines a trade secret as "technology information" or "business information" that is unknown to the public, valuable, and protected from disclosure by the rights-holder. In addition, China has labor, contract, and criminal laws that include trade secret-related provisions.[11]

A trade secret is the best protection when nondisclosure has great value. Contrast the trade secret with the patent. Patents require public disclosure, and the protection provided is for a limited duration. The formula for *Coca-Cola*®, for example, would now be in the public domain if protected only under patent laws. Trade secrets are also a good choice for intellectual property that may not be patentable subject matter, such as customer lists. It is also necessary to consider a trade secret if your intellectual property is related to a fast-moving field, as it would be unwise to invest significant funds in patenting an invention that may be obsolete even before the patent issues.

One of the disadvantages of the trade secret is that you have no protection against someone who independently discovers it. For example, if competitors of the Kentucky Fried Chicken franchise discover the Colonel's secret recipe by experimenting on their own, they are fully entitled to use their discovery without restriction.

Patents

A patent is an exclusive right granted for an invention, which is a product or a process that provides a new way of doing something or that offers a new technical solution to a problem.[12] The government issues the patent to the inventor or the inventor's assignee, and usually excludes others from making, using, or selling the invention for a limited time in exchange for public disclosure of the invention. Patents are, in essence, time-restricted legal monopolies. In most countries, to qualify for patent protection an invention must be novel (new), non-obvious to a person with ordinary skill in the art of the invention, and useful.

Patentable subject matter covers a broad range of inventions—from genetically modified mice (Harvard's OncoMouse)[13] to a cow urine and antibiotic mixture (Indian Gomutra).[14] But many categories are not protectable, such as natural phenomena (even if you discover it), printed matter (look to copyright instead), abstract ideas, and scientific principles. In 2013, the US Supreme Court decided that isolating a genetic DNA sequence is not entitled to protection, calling into question the validity of many previously issued patents.[15] However for non-patentable subject matter, there is still the possibility of legal protection through copyrights, trademarks, and trade secrets.

A common misconception about patent protection is that the grant is an exclusive right for the inventor to use the invention. A patent is actually not a right of the inventor to use the invention, but a right to exclude others from use. Imagine that you own an automobile but do not have a driver's license. You cannot drive the car yourself, but as long as you have the keys, no one else can drive it. Also, as long as you have the keys, you can decide who may use the automobile. With a patent, the inventor is the automobile owner and decides who will receive the keys and drive the automobile through use permissions such as licensing.[16]

A similar misconception relates to the words "patent pending"—a term that you may see occasionally on products. It is important to know that a patent filing per se doesn't offer any protection, but it does serve as a warning to competitors that if the patent issues, their use will potentially be infringement. Marking an item as patent pending is therefore a good strategy to limit competition from other companies.

There are many famous patents worldwide—the bread toaster, the smartphone, the aerosol spray can. From Whitney's cotton gin to Intel's microprocessors, protected inventions revolutionize our way of life and provide their creators with benefits. This system of encouraging innovation through the grant of a "patent"—like other intellectual property protection—is believed to be thousands of years old.

According to Kenneth W. Dobyns in *The Patent Office Pony: A History of the Early Patent Office* (1997), protecting innovation was seen for the first time around 500 B.C. in a Greek colony known as Sybaris. The Sybarites, who

> enjoyed living in luxury, made a law that if any confectioner or cook should invent any peculiar and excellent dish, no other artist was allowed to make this dish for one year. He who invented it was entitled to all the profit to be derived from the manufacture of it for that time. This was done in order that others might be induced to labor at excelling in such pursuits.

In addition to encouraging creativity, this culinary patent was a clever business strategy in that it attracted curious and wealthy visitors looking to experience the luxurious Sybarite culture.

In the United States, three types of patents may be granted to an inventor: (1) utility patent, (2) design patent, and (3) plant patent.

The utility patent may be issued for a new and useful machine, process, article of manufacture, or composition of matter (or improvement). The term of this form of patent is twenty years from the filing date. Utility patents make up the majority of the approximately eight million patents that have been issued by the US Patent and Trademark Office. The patentable subject matter included in this protection is quite broad. Examples include the popular board game *Monopoly*, Alexander Graham Bell's telephone (thought to be the most valuable patent in history), and Clarence Birdseye's process for packaging frozen food.[17]

The design patent may be granted for a new, original, and ornamental design for an article of manufacture. The term of this form of patent is fourteen years from the date of issuance (fifteen years for filings after May 13, 2015). Design patents protect the way an article looks. They have been issued for the Lamborghini Murciélago car design, the Rolex diving watch, and even for the shape of Frito-Lay's Wavy Lays potato chips.[18]

The plant patent may be issued for any distinct or new variety of plant generated through asexual reproductive methods. Sexually reproduced plants are not "made by man" and, for that reason, cannot be the subject of a patent. The term of this form of patent is twenty years from the filing date. This type is the rarest form of patent protection issued by the patent office, accounting for less than a third of 1% of patents granted annually. Some plant patents include the Bridal Pink™ Rose, *Royal Tioga* cherry tree, and the hundreds of seed patents owned by US corporations such as Monsanto.[19]

In the United States, there is rigorous patent enforcement and protection of the inventor's right to exclude. US patent laws trace their origin to Article I, section 8, clause 8 of the Constitution, intending to "promote the Progress of Science and useful Arts, by securing for limited Times to Authors and Inventors the exclusive Right to their respective Writings and Discoveries." Title 35 of the US Code is the modern statute that protects American inventors. The United States Patent and Trademark Office ("USPTO") grants patents, and these patent rights extend only throughout the United States. Because US patents have no effect in a foreign country, inventors interested in extending their invention protection in other countries must apply for a patent in each of the desired countries or in regional patent offices.

Internationally, the World Trade Organization's ("WTO") 1994 Agreement on Trade-Related Aspects of Intellectual Property Rights ("TRIPS") sets minimum standards for member countries with respect to the availability, scope, and use of intellectual property rights, including patent rights. All member countries—those that have signed the TRIPS agreement—are required to establish and enforce the minimum standards, although each country can institute more stringent requirements. The least-developed member countries, which require technical and financial assistance to achieve the TRIPS standards, were recently provided with an implementation extension until the year 2021. Through the TRIPS agreement, the WTO recognizes the importance of consistency in protecting and enforcing intellectual property in our globally-connected world.[20]

The application of TRIPS has helped build uniformity in worldwide patenting. For example, the majority of countries that issue patents now adhere to the twenty-year term of protection. And, in 2013, the United States moved closer to a long-standing international standard by transitioning from a "first to invent" to a "first inventor to file" system.

Under the old first-to-invent system, inventors could gain priority over competing patent applications by proving that they were the first to develop an invention. When there were conflicting claims between inventors, the patent office would declare an "interference" and hold a hearing. A famous American interference in the early 1880s involved a claim by inventors William E. Sawyer and Albon Man against Thomas Edison, all creators of the incandescent lamp. After much legal wrangling, US Patent 317,676 was granted to Sawyer and Man in 1883.[21] But in the recently-adopted first-to-file process, the first of competing inventors to file a patent application on the same invention usually receives priority.

Patenting is increasing globally at a phenomenal rate, with millions of patent applications filed worldwide every year. The process of obtaining a patent is known as "patent prosecution" and begins with filing an application that describes the invention in great detail. Inventors disclose not only how to make and use their inventions but also, in some countries, any related or similar types of inventions that may already exist—known as "prior art." The United States is among the small number of countries that require an affirmative duty of disclosure. For example, there was a US patent (No. 147,119) issued in 1874 for a combined eating utensil improvement—which later came to be known as a "spork"—and the prior art disclosed for this invention included the spoon, fork, and knife.[22]

The patent office receiving the application reviews the claims the inventor makes and, if the invention meets the statutory requirements, will grant the patent. Due to the complexity of patenting, it is wise to seek the help of a patent attorney. The United Kingdom patenting office estimates that only one in twenty inventors is able to succeed in obtaining a patent without an attorney's assistance. While the patent prosecution process can be lengthy and tedious, the average twenty years of protection for an invention can be advantageous.[23]

Patent protection, as opposed to trade secret protection, is best for inventions that can be "reverse-engineered" or otherwise easily discovered by others. Reverse engineering refers to the process by which you take apart an invention and figure out how it is made and operates. A patent discloses all the information that would be obtained through the reverse-engineering process, and prevents the potential reverse engineer from making or using the invention for a limited time.

The idea behind a patent is an equitable one—to give inventors time to profit from their work before others may do the same. However, the public disclosure requirement of patenting is a double-edged sword. Indeed, when everyone knows how to make your invention, someone will inevitably try to use or sell it before your protection ends. While the risk of possible infringement of your patent is one of the disadvantages of this form of protection over a trade secret, the patent does provide recourse against these interlopers. Accordingly, patent protection is also best for inventions in which infringement of the patent is readily detectable.

Trademarks

A trademark is a word, phrase, symbol, or design, or a combination thereof, that identifies and distinguishes the source of the goods of one party from those of others.[24] The name "Google" for example, is a trademark, and is considered to be the most valuable in the world with an estimated value of more than $100 billion.[25]

Other forms of marks also exist, including service marks, which distinguish the source of a service rather than goods. The golden arches of McDonalds' restaurants are an example of a service mark. There are also collective marks, which are used to identify members of an organization, such as the Girl Scouts of America, and certification marks, which identify products or services as meeting certain standards.[26]

A common international certification mark is the "CE mark," which indicates that a product complies with safety, health, or environmental requirements set by the European Commission. (CE stands for Communauté Européenne, which is French for "European Community.") "The CE mark is mandatory on certain products sold within the European Economic Area ("EEA"). The EEA comprises the twenty-eight member states of the European Union, the four member states of the European Free Trade Association (Iceland, Liechtenstein, Norway, and Switzerland), and Turkey."[27]

Even sounds can be trademarked (called "sound marks"). Famous sound marks include Apple's start-up chime for Mac computers,

Tarzan's yell, and Duracell Battery's three-note "coppertop" audio logo.[28] In 1994, the American motorcycle manufacturer Harley-Davidson tried to obtain a sound mark for its classic crankpin V-twin engine exhaust sound. This trademark application caused considerable concern among other manufacturers that their V-twin motorcycles might infringe on such a mark. After years of dogged pursuit in court, Harley-Davidson finally withdrew its application.[29]

Trademarks are often among the most valuable assets of a business. Trademarked symbols, logos, words, stylized letters, colors, sounds, motions, textures—and even scents—allow a business to build brand recognition in the marketplace. Therefore, to be valid, a trademark must be distinctive. The mark must allow consumers and other users to identify goods or services as being provided by a particular source.

The "Swoosh" of Nike® athletic shoes and products, for example, is considered the most recognizable branding trademark in the world. The swoosh was created by a graphic arts student in 1971, who was paid $35 for the design. At the time the mark was adopted, Nike co-founder Phil Knight said about the swoosh, "I don't love it, but I think it will grow on me."[30] The Nike company created value by "associating its trademark with a lifestyle and way of doing things that provided consumers with something meaningful to identify with," as the swoosh "stands for athleticism, power, fitness."[31] The swoosh features prominently in the $100 per second that the company spends on advertising each year. With more than $30 billion in annual sales, it is clear the company's trademark strategies have contributed greatly to Nike's success.[32]

The all-important distinctiveness requirement for trademarks separates marks into four categories: (1) fanciful (coined), (2) arbitrary, (3) suggestive, and (4) descriptive. Fanciful marks are considered to be the most distinctive and provide the trademark owner with the strongest protection. These marks are combinations of symbols or words that do not signify anything outside of the goods or services they are being used to identify. Xerox®, Kodak®, and Google® are examples of fanciful or coined marks. These types of marks provide the best protection because they are so distinctive. In the event of infringement or cybersquatting, owners will be in a strong position to argue the integrity of their mark. Google® was originally named "Backrub," presumably because the underlying algorithm counts backlinks. If Google founders Larry Page and Sergey Brin had decided to keep the name Backrub, it would likely be characterized as an arbitrary mark, and wouldn't provide the same level of protection as the fanciful Google®.[33, 34]

Arbitrary marks typically have a common meaning, but that meaning is not connected with the goods or services they represent. Arbitrary marks do not offer the same level of protection as the fanciful mark because they are not as distinctive.

The Apple® trademark is a good example of an arbitrary mark that has created some legal and use problems for the company. For nearly forty years, Apple Corps (the Beatles-founded record label and holding company) and Apple, Inc. (Apple computers) have been fighting over the use of the "Apple" trademark. Apple Corps has sued Apple, Inc. multiple times for trademark infringement based on the association of the word "Apple" with music-related materials. The most recent lawsuit focused on iTunes and iPod music and was settled in 2007 when the companies agreed that Apple, Inc. would own all the trademarks related to "Apple," and license the trademark back to the Beatles' Apple Corps. The Apple saga illustrates the concerns that arbitrary marks can create for holders.[35, 36]

Suggestive marks contain some attribute or benefit of the goods or services they represent, but do not describe the products themselves. For example, Microsoft® represents software for microcomputers, and Greyhound® is a bus transportation service.[37] Courts have said that a mark is suggestive if it requires imagination, thought, and perception to determine what the trademark represents.

An example of the protection, or lack thereof, afforded a suggestive mark is the 2002 case of *Thane International v. Trek Bicycle*. When the litigation began, Trek Bicycles had long used the trademark TREK and had associated the mark with more than a thousand products. When Thane began to use the trademark Orbitrek on its stationary bikes, Trek sued for infringement. The court found in favor of Thane:

> TREK is a suggestive mark because trek means a long journey, and one can undertake a long journey on a bicycle. As a suggestive mark, TREK has more distinctiveness than a merely descriptive mark and deserves some trademark protection. However, it does not belong to the highest category of distinctiveness, that reserved for arbitrary and fanciful marks, and thus does not deserve as much protection.

In most countries, descriptive marks are usually not protectable unless the public has come to recognize them as trademarks. These marks are said to have "acquired distinctiveness" or "secondary meaning." For example, the word "Sharp" is associated with televisions as a suggestive trademark. Yet even with secondary meaning, the descriptive mark is a weak mark with very narrow protection. This type of mark's lack of distinctiveness is frequently the source of disagreements between company marketing professionals and their legal departments. While marketers try to convey information about products and services by using descriptive terms, from the perspective of a legal strategy, these types of marks are difficult to enforce. Therefore, businesses should focus on the use of fanciful and arbitrary marks, which ensure the best trademark protection.

Another type of trademark protection that businesses may consider is known as "trade dress." This category is defined by the International Trademark Association as "the overall commercial image (look and feel) of a product that indicates or identifies the source of the product and distinguishes it from those of others." Trade dress may include product packaging, ornamental aspects, and even physical décor and environment that complement the "total visual image" of a company's products and/or services.

In 1992 there was a case of trade dress infringement before the US Supreme Court.[38] The restaurant chain Taco Cabana sued a similar eatery group, Two Pesos, for the latter's copycat use of bright colors, patio areas, and building paint schemes. The Court found in favor of Taco Cabana, stating that the restaurant's trade dress was inherently distinctive and entitled to protection. In the year following the decision, for which Taco Cabana received $3.7 million in damages, the twenty-nine existing Two Pesos restaurants were sold to Taco Cabana and promptly liquidated.[39]

Trademark rights are typically established through use in commerce or by a registration process. In legal systems based primarily on English common law, such as the United States, the United Kingdom, Hong Kong, and India, simply using a mark can establish rights. In some of these common law countries, the unregistered trademark may be enforced against an infringer through the tort of "passing off." This common law tort prevents one business from portraying its goods or services as being the goods and services of another business in a manner creating confusion in consumer markets.

An interesting defense that may be used by the party accused of "passing off" is the "moron in a hurry" test. This test was first used by British Justice Foster in a 1978 case in which the publishers of the *Morning Star*, a British Communist Party newspaper, sought to prevent Express Newspapers from launching a new tabloid, the *Daily Star*. The judge ruled against the *Morning Star*, noting that

"If one puts the two papers side by side, I for myself would find that the two papers are so different in every way that only a moron in a hurry would be misled."[40] Interestingly enough, Apple, Inc. used the "moron in a hurry" defense in one of the Beatles' Apple Corps lawsuits. Apple Inc.'s lawyers argued that "even a moron in a hurry could not be mistaken about" the difference between iTunes and the Beatles' Apple record label.[41]

Under a trademark registration system, a company may apply for more formal protection of trademarks used in commerce through a country's governmental trademark agency. In the United States, trademark registration begins with an application to the Patent and Trademark Office. The application provides evidence that the mark has been used in commerce or will be used within six months after the filing.

The initial trademark term is ten years, but the owner may renew the mark indefinitely provided it is still in use (although continued use is not required for renewal in every country). Some of the oldest registered trademarks include the Bass Brewery label in the United Kingdom (1876), the Samson Rope Technologies mark in the United States (1884), and the Krupp Steel Company mark in Germany (1875).[42] Provisions under TRIPS also set the international standard of a ten-year registration.

Certain symbols, such as ®, Reg., [TM], and [SM], are often attached to marks to show registration status. The symbols ® or Reg. may be associated with registration in one or more countries, while [TM] and [SM] are used for unregistered trademarks and service marks to indicate either protection under common law or pending formal registration. Other symbols include "Marca Registrada" or MR in some countries where Spanish is the dominant language, and "Marque Déposée" ("Marque de Commerce") or their abbreviations (MD and MC) in some countries where French is the dominant language.[43] Trademark registration symbols serve to place others on notice that there is a recognized right in the trademark—a right that the trademark holder is potentially ready to enforce.

The greatest advantage of trademark protection is the company's opportunity to safeguard its brand and reputation from potential counterfeiters and infringers. While misuse of trademarks may result in small lost profits, misuse can also ruin the trademark holder's reputation and cause business failure. One disadvantage of the trademark is the relatively weak nature of mark protection. This drawback should encourage businesses to concentrate on mark distinctiveness, which affords better protection than marks classified as fanciful or arbitrary.

Copyrights

A copyright is a form of protection granted by law for original works of authorship fixed in a tangible medium of expression. Copyright covers both published and unpublished works, and includes materials such as computer programs, musical compositions, broadcasts, sound recordings, films, and writings.[44]

Many people do not realize that a copyright instantly attaches to a work once it is expressed in a tangible medium. In many countries, you do not need to register a copyright unless you intend to seek damages for copyright infringement. The exclusive rights under a copyright typically include making copies of the work, distributing copies, controlling derivative works, and the right to attribution (being credited as the work's creator).

The duration of a copyright varies depending on the jurisdiction, but for most works it usually includes the life of the author plus 50 to 100 years. For example, the current copyright terms in Mexico, the United States, India, and China are, respectively, the author's life plus 100, 70, 60, and 50 years. If a country is a signatory to either the Berne Convention or the WTO's TRIPS agreement, the copyright term is a minimum of the author's life plus 50 years. Country member candidates for entrance into the European Union are required to set a term of life plus 70 years.[45]

After the copyright term expires, the work falls into the public domain, which means that anyone can copy, distribute, or otherwise use it. Recall the once-copyrighted "Happy Birthday to You" song mentioned earlier. Prior to September 2015, it was fine to sing the Happy Birthday song to a loved one in your dining room, but illegal to post a video of the song on YouTube or sing it at a restaurant unless a fee was paid to either the American Society of Composers, Authors and Publishers ("ASCAP") or the copyright holder. (ASCAP collects fees for public performances of many copyrighted works.)

Although holders of the copyright to the Happy Birthday song have collected around $50 million in licensing fees, a lawsuit filed in 2013 claimed the song is in the public domain. A federal judge ruled on September 22, 2015 that there is no evidence that a copyright claim to the Happy Birthday song is valid.[46] So, for anyone celebrating an upcoming birthday, feel free to sing away in the venue of your choosing, compliments of the US District Court for the Central District of California.

Copyright infringement situations are common. Of all the forms of intellectual property, copyright might be the most difficult to monitor and enforce against unauthorized use, due primarily to the vast number of protected works. From the millions of songs available, for example, a music digital download can be purchased and then multiple illegal copies produced from that single copy.

One of the most famous cases of copyright infringement involved the music industry in a 2001 case, *A&M Records v. Napster*. Around 2000, peer-to-peer ("P2P") file sharing increased at a phenomenal rate. A company known as Napster began an Internet website with technology that allowed people to share MP3 files with others very easily. At its peak, the group had eighty million registered users.[47]

In 2000, after several major musicians experienced unauthorized pre-release circulation of their music, bands and recording companies sued Napster for copyright infringement. Unable to prevail in court, Napster ceased operations in 2001 and declared bankruptcy in 2002. The company's assets were acquired initially by Roxio, then later by the online music subscription service Rhapsody. Although just one of many infringement cases in the music industry, the highly-publicized *Napster* case was one of the first to drive home the point that much of P2P sharing violated the law.[48]

Defenses to copyright infringement in the United States include the First Sale Doctrine and Fair Use rule. Under the First Sale Doctrine, the owner of a legally-obtained copy of a work is entitled to sell that copy. The doctrine does not, however, allow the legal owner to make and sell copies of the owned copy—or even to give them away. In limited circumstances, copyright law will allow a legal owner to make archival copies for personal use. For example, the law permits you to make a single copy of a legally-obtained computer software program in case the original is lost or damaged. But that back-up copy must be destroyed or transferred if you ever sell the original copy.

The Fair Use rule is a part of copyright law that allows for the limited use of copyrighted material without permission from the rights holder. Examples include the use of copyrighted material for commentary, parody, research, criticism, and teaching. Fair use may also apply to news reporting. In 2014, a US court confirmed that the news organization Bloomberg did not infringe copyright when it published a corporate earnings report phone call transcript and recording. The court said that because the publication had a newsworthy purpose, it qualified for a copyright exception under fair use.[49]

An example application of the fair use infringement defense is the case of *Whitmill v. Warner Brothers* involving the film "The Hangover Part II." In the movie, one of the characters has a facial tattoo that resembles the Maori design of boxing champion Mike Tyson's facial tattoo. Tyson played a role in the film. Tyson's tattoo artist, S. Victor Whitmill, sued Warner Brothers for violating his copyright in the design. Warner Brothers claimed that the depiction fell under the fair use exception as a parody, but before a full hearing could be scheduled the case settled and the film was released. Another issue in the case was whether Whitmill himself committed a copyright violation by stealing an original Maori design.[50]

If the fair use is for educational purposes, there is also a bit of leeway to use copyrighted material, although this is not a free pass to use such material without discretion. Even educators and librarians are cautioned to seek permission if there is extensive or prolonged use of copyrighted material. Not every country has a fair use exception to copyright. China has no equivalent to the exception, but Indian court decisions and British law allow limited fair use—termed "fair dealing"—for research, private study, criticism, and review.[51]

An additional defense to copyright infringement is the demonstration that material was developed in a "clean room." This is a process, often used by software companies, where individuals work independently without access to outside or third party sources. Developments in the clean room are not considered to be infringing on copyrighted material, even if substantially similar to existing sources.

One advantage of copyright protection is that it is the least expensive form of protection for eligible intellectual property. A benefit of a registered copyright is the ability to sue infringers and potentially collect significant damages, including profits earned and attorney fees. In 2010, a US District Court jury awarded the software company Oracle a record $1.3 billion in copyright infringement damages from the technical support service group SAP.[52] Although the amount of the monetary award was later reduced, without registered copyright protection Oracle would have had difficulty obtaining a remedy for SAP's infringement. Given the minimal time, fees, and effort required to file for a copyright, you should strongly consider using this form of IP protection.

The Law Pillar: Intellectual Property Risk Management

You might be familiar with the American chocolate wafer and cream cookie once called *Hydrox* that is rumored to have evolved into the Nabisco brand Oreo®. The Hydrox™ cookie was marketed beginning in 1908, but then withdrawn from the market in 2008. Leaf Brands, a company that revives disappeared food items, decided to bring Hydrox™ back. However, there was an obstacle— the US-based company Kellogg owned the cookie's trademark.

Leaf Brands knew that if a company is not using a trademark, you can in essence "steal" it by asking the USPTO for permission to use it. The only caveat is you must provide the trademark office evidence that the current trademark owner is not using the trademark and has no future plans to use it. So Leaf Brands cleverly wrote to Kellogg's consumer affairs office, explaining that it was a fan of the cookie, and asking, "Do you have any plans to bring it back?" Kellogg replied "Sorry—no plans to ever revive the Hydrox™ brand." Shortly thereafter, Leaf Brands received permission from the USPTO to use the Hydrox™ trademark.[53]

The Leaf Brands example illustrates the need to protect your company's intellectual property. What follows are both general and specific legal strategies for safeguarding IP assets.

General Strategies

The best general IP protection strategies focus on strong offensive and defensive approaches. Two possibilities are described in Michael Gollin's book *Driving Innovation* (2008) on international IP strategies: the Burning Stick strategy and the Suit of Armor and Shield strategy.

The offensive Burning Stick strategy is especially relevant to small-sized and medium-sized enterprises that are organizing their IP portfolios amid an eat-or-be-eaten competitive jungle. These organizations need to build a campfire to ward off "wild animals"—competitors, and others who might hinder their success. Gollin says the fire doesn't need to be big, but it should be strong—including vigorous protection of key assets that companies identify as vital to their goals. You should apply for patents and mark products as "patent-pending." You should fortify trade secret protections with restricted access—for example, the only-two-executives rule of Coca-Cola and Kentucky Fried Chicken. Air-tight confidentiality agreements should accompany even the smallest disclosure of proprietary information.

All copyrightable materials—company newsletters, advertising materials, training manuals—are noted as such. Important copyrights are registered and marked with a © symbol or the word "Copyright." Even though using the copyright symbol is no longer required to enforce your rights under the Berne Convention (an international treaty), it still serves to warn potential infringers. All valuable trademarks, especially those associated with key assets, should be registered and marked on all literature, packaging, and websites.

Any infringement is addressed through a cease-and-desist letter, which is usually enough to discourage further violations. If the infringement persists, the company may threaten litigation—but it is wise to seek more conservative avenues first, such as licensing arrangements. Although this highly vigilant strategy appears aggressive, it will place the company in a strong position to move forward in creating value for its IP assets.

The second possible strategy, Suit of Armor and Shield, adds a defensive component to the Burning Stick approach. The company in this scenario suits up like a warrior in battle to face the army of IP-holding competitors. As Sun Tzu said in *The Art of War*, "Victorious warriors win first and then go to war, while defeated warriors go to war first and then seek to win."

Preparation is the key to this strategy. Conduct Freedom to Operate Analyses ("FTOs") on your key assets, which is the process of determining whether an action, such as commercializing a product, will infringe on the IP rights of others. This information serves as a risk management tool to minimize and plan around potential infringing activities. There are many services that will conduct these studies for you, and for very important assets you may secure an FTO opinion from an experienced patent attorney.

Although the FTO opinion may be costly, it can support your defense in an infringement suit. The FTO is especially important for company products or services that are entering a highly competitive market dominated by big industry players (with deep pockets to support infringement litigation). Knowing what the competition is doing will also help identify infringement on *your* company's holdings. Even if you do not act on competitor infringement immediately, you should keep it in reserve to form the basis for counterclaims, in case you are sued at a later date. The stickier the situation becomes, the more likely all parties will settle through low-key negotiation or mediation, as opposed to expensive litigation.

Specific Strategies: Trade Secrets

The key to trade secret success is maintaining strict confidentiality in the IP asset. Because trade secret protection can be lost when companies fail to take reasonable efforts to maintain secrecy, a company's conduct is at the core of this IP form. The first reasonable effort a company can take is to educate employees about the importance and nature of trade secret protection, and to require each individual to sign an agreement that addresses confidentiality and IP ownership. Customers, independent contractors, consultants, and even volunteers and interns should also sign agreements outlining permissible use of proprietary information. Physical and computer security measures should be rigorous. Online postings should be scrutinized carefully so that confidential information is not inadvertently exposed—because once the trade secret is disclosed, whether accidental or otherwise, the protection for that asset ends and can never be revived.

One of the limitations of trade secret protection is the potential for reverse engineering. If an asset can be reversed engineered easily, a patent may be the wiser form of protection. Google's mix of invention trade secrets and patents illustrates this strategy well. For example, the PageRank link analysis algorithm process is patented, while PageRank manipulation tools are trade secrets.[54]

Another strategy for protecting the trade secret is to employ technical obstructions, such as black box components, to prevent reverse engineering. This strategy depends on the design and scope of the material being protected and can offer some obstacles on the road to independent discovery.

Specific Strategies: Patents

Patenting is a very strong form of protection for inventions. In addition to encouraging creativity (US President Abraham Lincoln said the patent "added the fuel of interest to the fire of genius"[55]), the enforcement system has spurred specific strategies that take full advantage of patenting logistics.

For example, International Business Machines ("IBM") ranks as one of the most innovative organizations in the world, reflected in the thousands of patents the company receives every year. Like all the big tech players, IBM patents core technologies and rigorously protects its inventions. But the company also uses strategies designed to extend their protection well beyond the essential focus of the primary patent.

One of these strategies is known as the "Picket Fence." In the usual picket fence approach, a company patents all of the incremental innovations surrounding the main invention. This ancillary protection forms a fence or blanket around the core technology and prevents other companies from building IP that can compete with the protected asset.

But IBM's picket fence strategy has a twist. Instead of patenting all the peripheral inventions, the company publishes them. Once available to the public, these small associated features of the core patent become "prior art" (recall the spork invention) and cannot be patented. So, in addition to saving the cost of non-core patenting, IBM prevents competitors from patenting around their primary innovation.[56]

Modern and historic patent infringement litigation is a serious issue. In recent years, Samsung and Apple have engaged in a patent infringement war over their respective smartphones. Both companies dominate the mobile phone market and are responsible for more than half the phones sold worldwide. At issue are claims of infringement of both companies' utility and design patents, trademarks, and other intellectual property. Fifty lawsuits have been filed in ten countries in the Samsung–Apple conflict. But the litigation on smartphone technology is not limited to Samsung and Apple, as Google, HTC, HUAWEI, Microsoft, Motorola, Nokia, and Sony have also either sued or been sued in smartphone and tablet patent skirmishes.[57]

WIPO estimates that the average patent infringement case in the United States costs a company between $3 million and $10 million, and takes two to three years to litigate. Such conflicts are unfortunately not new. For example, by the year 1896, there were more than 300 patent suits pending between early radio broadcasting giants General Electric and Westinghouse.[58]

There are some specific strategies companies can take to avoid this type of combat. For example, they can seek a licensing or cross-licensing arrangement for the IP that is at the center of the controversy. This strategy benefits the parties by both ending the expense of litigation and creating the potential to generate profits.

Similarity in products/IP portfolios might also form a basis for merger and acquisition activity. In the late 1990s two American companies, TV Guide and Gemstar, were close competitors and the only providers of interactive programming guides for dominant digital formats. After long-term patent litigation between them, these companies made the decision to merge. The result was a new company and a $14.2 billion stock deal. This pleased shareholders much more than the continued expense of litigation.[59] So, while some strategies may begin in adversity, there is always room at the negotiating table for a favorable settlement.

Specific Strategies: Trademarks

Patents and trade secrets are like the internal unseen bones of a company's intellectual property, whereas trademarks are the face of the company that is making the actual connection with the user and consumer. Branding is therefore a critical strategy for growing a company and gaining recognition in the marketplace. A great advantage of the trademark, mentioned earlier, is indefinite registration renewal. Like a trade secret, trademark protection can theoretically extend for eternity.

Before adopting a new mark, the company should search trademark databases (that's TESS in the United States—Trademark Electronic Search System) and be certain that the mark is available. Lack of knowledge is normally not a defense to trademark infringement, and it is also better to avoid wasting your investment if the trademark is already registered.

Some companies will focus on a trademark strategy that registers multiple related marks, forming a trademark cluster. The National Football League ("NFL"), for example, has created a trademark cluster around the phrase "Super Bowl®." The League has registered the Super Bowl® phrase for television broadcasting services, promotional materials, clothing, entertainment services, and Super Bowl® concerts. This cluster allows the NFL to control virtually every commercial aspect of the trademark in every venue.[60]

A trademark portfolio may also include registered domain names that can extend a company's brand throughout the online community. While most generic top-level domain names are relatively inexpensive, there are a few that have garnered top dollar such as insurance.com, which sold for over $35 million in 2010.[61]

The most effective strategies for trademarks are prompt registration, use of trademark symbols, and monitoring renewals. Failure to renew trademarks and pay fees can potentially result in losing trademark protection. To ensure maximum legal protection, do not forget the importance of "distinctiveness" as it relates to the four trademark categories.

Specific Strategies: Copyright

Like trademarks, prompt copyright registration is important if your business plans to enforce the rights in infringement actions. All transfers of copyright ownership must be in writing; oral transfers are not valid. Therefore, any outside consultants your company hires—website designers, copywriters, advertising professionals—should sign written copyright assignments. Clear and documented understanding of who owns the various rights in the copyright bundle should be a priority for all companies.

Copyright may be provided to the many writings important to a company, including annual public company reports, computer software programs (make sure to keep the copyright of an outside programmer's work in the name of the company), customer and mailing lists stored on a computer, product drawings and technical schematics, instructional manuals, promotional materials, and logos. As with any intellectual property, copyrights should be monitored carefully for infringement, especially in light of the ease in which violations occur via the Internet.

As mentioned, companies should keep in mind defenses to infringement, such as fair use and the clean room strategy. Documentation is the key to supporting authorized use in case the company is challenged in its use of copyrighted material.

Companies should be aware that there are different ways to both own and share copyright. Depending on what a company hopes to accomplish with its most valuable copyrights, it may decide to commit some rights to outlets such as Shareware or the Creative Commons. The copyright owner decides what rights, if any, are offered to these sources and may require attribution or place limitations on use. Tim O'Reilly of O'Reilly Media wrote that "Obscurity is a far greater threat to authors and creative artists than piracy,"[62] and this sentiment often holds true for other corporate copyrighted material as well. While there might not be a direct profit from sharing copyright with open sources, benefits can be garnered indirectly through enhanced distribution and marketing.

It is also important for a company to think outside the box, and consider nontraditional forms of expression that can be protected. For example, you can take as many photographs as you like of Paris' Eiffel Tower in the daytime and post them online. The nighttime lighting of the tower, however, is copyrighted, and anyone posting these images is expected to remit a licensing fee to the French government.[63]

Aligning the Strategy Pillar with the Law Pillar by Using Intellectual Property to Create Value

In the American film *The Matrix*, the character Morpheus offers newcomer Neo a choice between two pills—one blue, one red. The blue pill offers a continued, but comfortable, lack of awareness, and the red pill offers a gateway to a new reality. "The Matrix is everywhere. It is all around us. Even now in this very room; you can see it when you look out the window, or turn on the television…." Neo takes the red pill and soon comes to better understand the Matrix, with all its associated risks and rewards.

Developing and maintaining intellectual property is like taking the red pill. Once you begin to become aware of assets that are both unique to your business and protectable as intellectual property, a whole new world emerges. Whereas safeguarded intellectual property assets range from the mundane to the spectacular, nearly each and every one will provide an advantage to companies that hold them. And although identifying, protecting, and monitoring intellectual property assets might be costly and risky, the costs and risks of doing nothing are often much greater.

Designing the Intellectual Property Management Plan

Once you are familiar with the forms of intellectual property and their associated responsibilities, it is time to form a strategic plan within your company to maximize IP asset use and create value for your investors. One of the best routes to create a strategy is to take the following steps: (1) review existing goals, (2) identify assets, (3) evaluate the competition, and (4) develop a plan.[64]

Review Existing Goals. You cannot plan a trip well if you do not know where you are going. Preparing an IP strategy for a company requires understanding what the business seeks to do, or where it hopes to be, in the future. For example, one of Google's long-term goals is to be the best and most user-friendly search engine available on the Internet. To achieve this objective, Google works continuously on its search engine technology. The company makes around five hundred to six hundred improvements to its patents and trade secrets every year.[65] But before founders of Google protected any inventions, researched what their competitors were doing, or developed a strategy, they wisely established the strategic goal of being the greatest search engine in existence.[66] Once you know where your company is headed, you can identify the IP assets that will take you there.

Identify Assets. Many businesses believe that only big industry players, such as Samsung and Apple, hold valuable intellectual property. This myth keeps small-sized and medium-sized enterprises from evaluating their IP inventories. This, in turn, prevents these companies from developing strategies to create value. Some IP assets are "hidden in plain sight" around you. That's why the next step in building an IP strategy is to identify these assets. They might include obvious ones among the main categories we have already discussed: trademarks, patents, copyrights, and trade secrets. They also might include less-recognized assets such as custom software, formulations, training manuals and other publications, licenses, branding, distribution contracts, client lists, product certifications, franchise agreements, drawings, promotional literature, raw material networks, know-how—and the list can go on and on.

An initial IP audit will be akin to Dorothy stepping out into the Technicolor wonderland of MGM's 1939 film *The Wizard of Oz*—things will never be the same. Various publications can provide a company with intellectual property assessment instruments; information about each asset should include aspects such as product life, extent of use, importance, and estimated value. You should inventory policies already in place, as well as the human resources needed to support existing assets. Very important assets can benefit from IP valuation.

Evaluate the Competition. Once you have surveyed the intellectual property landscape, you are ready to assess competition. Assessing other companies' rights, and how they have protected and exercised those rights, is important to understanding your internal IP prospects. For example, firms in the biotechnology field struggle with a "patent thicket" of overlapping rights that tends to result in what is known as the stacking of licensing royalties.

Because biotech research involves so many closely related methods and processes, there are often multiple patent licenses and other rights that need to be secured before a new invention investigation can move forward. In this situation, a freedom to operate analysis, where the protected intellectual property of competitors is evaluated, is useful in preventing potential infringement. If a blocking protected right is discovered, options include assessing whether the competitor's IP is valid and, if so, cross-licensing or inventing around the existing property.

Awareness of competitor IP portfolios can also be a form of benchmarking. Author Michael Gollin in *Driving Innovation* provides the example of a brewing company with a vast array of trademarks but few patents in its portfolio compared to other brewers. Based on this information, the brewer can decide whether to increase its own patenting activities, seek to purchase existing patents, or choose other ways to strengthen its position within the industry. Awareness of competitors' IP and how they are using it helps you organize your holdings, avoid infringement, and gain a competitive edge in the marketplace.

Develop a Plan. Once a company is aware of its intellectual property and has evaluated and cataloged its portfolio, the next step is to develop a plan to maximize IP protection, use, and value in line with organizational goals. This step is accomplished by examining the company's individual assets, and developing a strategy for each. Some of the plans and strategies will be simple, such as copyrighting and marking blog entries or promotional literature. Other plans will be more complex, and potentially expensive, combining multiple forms of protection and vigilant infringement monitoring.

Forming an IP strategy has tremendous benefits. When a plan is formulated and implemented, managers can look forward to increased revenues, growing brand recognition, and added attention from investors. Companies can employ numerous strategies, some of which were covered earlier in this chapter, to set the IP management plan in motion and create value in the identified assets. Managers should consider the nature of their company's assets, and select strategies that align with organizational goals.

One example of a successful concentrated IP plan involves the NFL's trademark of the words Super Bowl®, mentioned earlier. The Super Bowl® event marks the season end of one of America's most popular sports. The NFL first began using the term in 1969 and has held the trademark for many years. Throughout its ownership period, the football league has been aggressive in enforcing the Super Bowl® trademark. A team of attorneys monitors every use of the mark for infringement and unauthorized use. NFL enforcers even closed down a church's game viewing party because congregants used the Super Bowl® trademark in advertising the event.

This "super" vigilance is related to two factors. First, trademark holders must pursue infringers to maximize their damage recovery in court actions. Second, the Super Bowl® trademark is especially valuable. With sponsors paying tens of millions of dollars for the privilege of using the football league's intellectual property, the NFL's well-planned and executed protection of the Super Bowl® trademark is essential.[67]

Patents, like trademarks, can be a significant source of value for patent holders, although there might be gaps in the protection they offer. Not every company resorts to IBM's picket fence around their inventions, due primarily to time and cost. A lack of broad protection can allow others to employ an "invent around" strategy. By studying a patent or published patent application's technology, you might be able to identify weaknesses or areas where an improvement can be developed. This approach can be as simple as changing just one element in the claims supporting a patent. Although the strategy can be tricky because you risk infringement, it can also be advantageous because much of the research and development heavy lifting is already completed. Author Gollin terms these invent around strategies patent "jiu-jitsu," because the process involves elements of good timing, skill, and agility.

Among the most critical strategies to create value from patents is licensing. The annual revenue attributed to licensing agreements in the United States is more than $500 billion.[68] Cross-licensing between companies of their IP holdings is common. Some entities will patent or otherwise protect IP that they would not otherwise use so that these assets are available as bargaining chips for negotiating licenses on assets others hold.

This strategy should not be confused with the actions of holding companies known as "patent trolls." Like other non-practicing entities, patent trolls acquire patents but rarely license the invention, manufacture products, or supply services related to the patents they own. Instead, the companies subsist on bringing infringement suits against others for violations of their patent holdings. In the United States, more than half the states have enacted anti-trolling laws, and federal legislation that places some limitations on patent trolling has been proposed.

Licensing strategies can also enable parties to avoid litigation, as illustrated by an IP dispute between the nation of Ethiopia and the coffee company Starbucks. According to the WIPO, coffee is the second most traded commodity after oil, and global citizens drink more than 400 billion cups each year. In 2004, the Ethiopian Intellectual Property Office attempted to register three trademarks on coffee beans in key market countries. The trademark applications were quickly opposed by the USPTO and by Starbucks as being too "generic" to qualify for registration. Starbucks tried to steer Ethiopia toward obtaining certification marks and foregoing trademarks, but the country held its position.

What began in an adversarial stance, however, ended in an alliance, due in part to Ethiopia's strategy of offering royalty-free licenses to foreign coffee distributors. The free licenses were intended to encourage large foreign coffee agents to promote and build recognition for Ethiopian products. Ethiopia's strategy of providing incentives and working cooperatively to accomplish its objectives created a win-win situation for all involved.[69]

Intellectual property holders can also cooperate by forming a patent pool. A patent pool is a grouping of intellectual property rights with the intent of cross-licensing. Patent pools have been formed to end legal wrangling (sewing machines, the movie industry), simplify manufacturing (Davoplane/Pullman folding beds), facilitate information gathering (railroads), fuel war efforts (aircraft manufacturers), seek global industry domination (radio), and protect/promote standards bodies (MPEG-2, DVD technology).[70] These patent rights consortiums have also been considered for computer software and biotechnology with the intent of eliminating or minimizing the cumulative effect of patent thickets.

A well-organized and administered patent pool can be advantageous for all participants by reducing litigation (think Samsung–Apple) and transaction costs, and by enabling companies that contribute to the pool to increase profits. Provided the pools do not become anticompetitive, they are a viable collective strategy for modern businesses.

The patent term is relatively short when compared to other forms of IP protection. But there are a few strategies to extend the life of a patent even after the specified term ends. One method is by "evergreening," which pharmaceutical companies commonly use to prolong their presence in the market. Evergreening involves patenting minor improvements or associated discoveries, and then associating the changes with established brand names already in the marketplace. A related strategy is transitioning patent protection to an emphasis on trademarks through intense advertising and marketing close to the time of patent expiration. The goal is to encourage consumers to continue buying products associated with the established "name" even when competing products are available.

Strategies for the Future

Michael Gollin notes in *Driving Innovation* that "the IP system is global in reach, and local in impact," requiring a balance between exclusive rights and access. There's no doubt that the world of intellectual property is complex and rapidly changing. Imbalance will exist, yet so will continued efforts to bring IP to sustainability. The company that takes steps to determine its goals, identify and protect its assets, evaluate competition, and develop a strategic plan for managing intangible assets will be in the best position as the modern age advances. Microsoft founder Bill Gates once said that "intellectual property has the shelf life of a banana."[71] But in a world of strategically-managed IP, a few days on the shelf may be all the time you need.

Key Takeaways

In a world where 70% of business assets are intangible, a company's ability to create, protect, and use intellectual property is the key to creating value and attracting investors. Value creation requires that you should:

1. **Become legally savvy about intellectual property law.** At a minimum, you should understand the four key categories of IP rights described in this chapter: trade secrets, patents, trademarks, and copyrights. You should also understand basic variations in these rights from country to country.

2. **Manage intellectual property risks.** You should consider general strategies such as the offensive Burning Stick and the defensive Suit of Armor and Shield strategies. You should also use strategies that relate to specific types of intellectual property. To protect your trade secrets, for example, you should educate employees about the nature of trade secret protection and require them to sign confidentiality agreements.

3. **Use intellectual property law to create value, which will attract investment to your company.** An IP management plan is key to creating value for your company. As part of your plan, you should review existing goals, identify IP assets, evaluate your competitors' IP, and align your IP strategy with your company's strategic goals.

III DEVELOP PROCESSES THAT BENEFIT ALL STAKEHOLDERS

6 Develop Contracts That Create Value for Both Sides

Part II of this book links key stakeholders with the most important legal risks affecting business: customers and product liability (Chapter 2), employees and employment law (Chapter 3), the government and regulatory law (Chapter 4), and investors and intellectual property (Chapter 5). In Part III, we now turn to the two remaining top legal risks that recent surveys have identified: contracts (in this chapter) and dispute resolution (Chapter 7). These risks involve processes that affect all stakeholders.

Any business, whether a startup or a major international corporation, relies on a web of contracts with stakeholders that include creditors, customers, employees, investors, and suppliers. As a result, business leaders must understand the fundamentals of contract law that are covered in the next section. The chapter will then turn to the Law Pillar and managing contract risks. The final section of the chapter aligns the Strategy Pillar with the Law Pillar by examining lean contracting and contract visualization.

Legal Briefing on Contracts

Perspectives on Contract Law

In essence, a contract is an agreement that is enforceable by law. We all enter into many agreements that are not legally enforceable. For example, you and I can strongly agree that a certain movie is the worst one we have ever seen, but our agreement is not enforceable in court. Contract law provides a framework for determining which of our agreements are enforceable.

Three perspectives are useful when thinking about contract law. First, there is a global perspective. In the global world of business, the rule of law is critically important when making business decisions. No legal rules are more important than contract law because contracts establish your rights and duties in business deals. Your first question when making investments in any country should be: Will my contract rights be respected and enforced in this country?

Second, from a company perspective, contracts are the key to business success. All other company activities—accounting, marketing, finance, strategy, and so on—are futile if your contracts are not profitable. Within companies, value is created during contract negotiations. And companies can fail when these negotiations do not produce successful results.

Third, from a personal perspective, contracts (both written and unwritten) permeate our daily lives. Whether these contracts involve the simple purchase of a meal or more complex transactions such as buying a house, they represent an important aspect of our interactions with other humans.

Because contracts are so common in our business and personal lives, we need a fundamental understanding of the sources of contract law and the four key elements that determine whether a contract has been formed. We now turn to these topics.

Understand the Sources of Contract Law

When you are involved in a negotiation and a contract law question arises, where can you find the answer? Two key questions determine the source of contract law. First, are you in civil law country or common law country? Second, what type of contract are you negotiating?

Type of Legal System. Although contract law in a globalized economy has become increasingly similar from country to country, differences still exist. The industrialized world is split between countries that have a civil law system and those with a common law system. Before beginning any contract negotiation, you should know which system governs your contract.

Generally, civil law countries include continental European countries and the former colonies of these countries. In civil law countries, the principles of law are found primarily in a "code"—in effect an encyclopedia of law. In contrast, common law countries (generally England and its former colonies) rely more heavily on previously-decided cases—that is, "precedents"—as a source of law.

The distinction between civil law and common law countries is especially important because the legal requirements for a valid contract differ in some ways between the systems. For example, civil law does not include the consideration requirement discussed in the next section.

Apart from differences in legal requirements, some practitioners have observed that common law contracts are lengthier because lawyers attempt to anticipate every possible scenario that might arise when a contract is performed. Civil law contracts, in contrast, are shorter because the contracts can simply refer to provisions from the code. Even in civil law countries, however, there is a trend toward longer contracts because the two systems often blend together when negotiations cross national borders.

Type of Contract. The second variable relating to the source of contract law requires understanding the type of contract you are negotiating. For example, let's assume that you manufacture golf equipment. I am negotiating the purchase of 100 putters, which I want to sell in my store. We reach an agreement on all the details except the price. Do we have a contract?

Under traditional common law, which governs the sale of real estate and services, price was a key element in forming a contract. However, our contract involves what lawyers call the sale of "goods." In the United States, the Uniform Commercial Code or, as it is commonly called in business negotiations, the UCC, governs the sale of goods. The UCC has modernized contract law. For example, if you intend to form a contract but have not said anything about price, the UCC provides that "the price is a reasonable price at the time of delivery" of the putters.

The situation becomes more complicated if you are negotiating an international contract. The good news is that eighty-one countries, including the United States, have ratified a treaty called the United Nations Convention on Contracts for the International Sale of Goods (known in business circles as the CISG). A uniform international sales law is a tremendous achievement that facilitates international trade.

The bad news is that some of the rules in the CISG differ from the UCC. For example, some experts have concluded that under the CISG the price must be stated or the contract must include a provision for determining the price.[1]

Use a Four-Part Contract Checklist

We now turn to the four key elements necessary to create a legally-enforceable contract. These elements represent a checklist for you to use in your future contract negotiations.

1. Reach an Agreement. The requirement that parties reach an agreement is fairly straightforward. One party makes an offer; the other party accepts the offer.

In many cases, common sense dictates whether a contract has been formed, as illustrated by facts adapted from a case in China. Let's assume that on Monday a store sent an offer to purchase televisions to a manufacturer, with delivery to be made to the store. On Wednesday, the manufacturer sent a reply accepting the offer but added that the store had to pick up the televisions at the factory. On Friday, the store agreed to this change. When the price of televisions dropped, the store claimed that there was no contract. Is there a contract?

Monday: Offers to buy TVs; delivery to store

Store   Manufacturer

Wednesday: Accepts offer, but store to pick up at plant

Friday: Store says OK

A common sense analysis is that the store made an offer on Monday, but the manufacturer's so-called "acceptance" was not a legal acceptance because it revised the terms of the offer by changing the place of delivery. This made the manufacturer's communication a counteroffer, which legally is a rejection of the offer. The store accepted the counteroffer on Friday, which created a contract. (For reasons too complicated to address here, under the UCC, acceptance possibly occurred on Wednesday. But in any event there is a contract.)

Preliminary documents. Negotiators often use a preliminary document during contract negotiations. This type of document (often called a memorandum of understanding, a memorandum of agreement, a letter of intent, or an agreement in principle) is a useful negotiating tool in complex negotiations when the two sides have difficulty reducing their negotiated agreement into writing. Even in a simple negotiation, such as renting an apartment, a pre-printed lease is a useful tool for converting a negotiation into a legal agreement.

Using preliminary documents carries a major risk, however. If the parties do not state clearly that they are not legally bound until a final contract is signed, a court might conclude that the documents have morphed into a binding contract as they became more detailed.

This risk might also affect third parties. For example, several years ago Pennzoil negotiated a memorandum of agreement to acquire Getty Oil. When Texaco later entered into a separate contract to purchase Getty Oil, Pennzoil claimed that its memorandum of agreement was actually a binding contract and that Texaco's actions interfered with Pennzoil's contract rights. In a subsequent trial, the jury agreed with Pennzoil in deciding that Texaco owed $10.5 billion in damages.

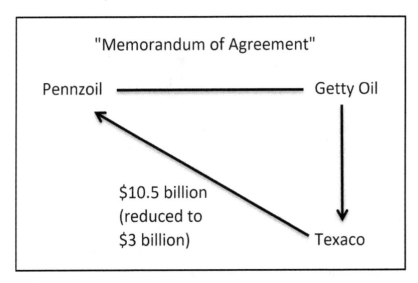

This was the largest verdict ever to be upheld on appeal. When this judgment drove Texaco into bankruptcy, the two companies reached a settlement agreement whereby Texaco paid Pennzoil "only" $3 billion. The Pennzoil attorney later recounted: "We celebrated that night [after winning the case] at my house by eating hamburgers and drinking beer. I've still got the $3 billion deposit slip on my wall."[2]

2. Give Up Something as Consideration. Consideration is a common law requirement. While consideration has a technical legal definition, in everyday language it means that for a deal to be legally binding, both sides must give up something. For example, if a graduate promises to donate $20 million to her university in a written, signed agreement, the agreement is generally not binding unless the university promises to give up something in return.

In most business transactions consideration is not a concern because both sides promise to give up something. One side promises to provide a service or a product and the other side promises to make payment.

However, the risk of not meeting the consideration requirement increases when a contract is modified. Let's assume that you, as a contractor, promise to remodel a building for a customer by a certain date and the customer promises to pay you $30,000. The two promises represent your mutual consideration.

At your request, the customer promises in writing to give you a one-month extension, but you do not give the customer anything in exchange for this extension. Technically, the customer's promise is not binding unless you provide additional consideration for the one-month extension.

3. Stay Within the Law. A contract that calls for violating a law is not enforceable. In many cases—for example, a contract to sell illegal drugs—this element is uncomplicated and easy to understand. In other situations, when a public policy might be violated, the law is more complex.

For example, your company might decide to protect confidential information by adopting a policy that requires current employees to sign so-called non-compete agreements. These agreements state that the employees cannot work for a competitor within three years after leaving your company.

States differ on the legality, and therefore the enforceability, of these non-compete agreements. In some states these agreements might be illegal because they restrict the ability of your employees to obtain employment. Even where the agreement is legal, in common law countries the consideration element would require your company to give something to current employees in exchange for requiring them to sign the non-compete agreement.

4. Put Your Agreement in Writing. Writing requirements raise important and complex concerns during negotiations. Both civil law and common law countries have rules providing that certain contracts must be in writing. Here are some typical examples of contracts that must be in writing under US law:

- Contracts for the sale of real estate
- Promises to pay the debts of others
- Agreements by an executor or administrator of an estate
- Promises made in exchange for a promise to marry
- Agreements that cannot be performed within one year
- Sales of goods for $500 or more

These rules carry a huge financial risk when you make an incorrect assumption about whether your agreement must be in writing. For example, you might miss a business opportunity because you thought that your oral agreement was binding when, in fact, the law requires a written contract. Or you might create an unintended liability because you thought that your oral agreement was not binding in a situation where the contract did not legally have to be in writing.

As a result, you should never enter into contract negotiations without understanding the rules about whether writing is required. Your understanding of the law should be supplemented by a practical strategy: when negotiating important contracts, make it clear that you are not bound until a written agreement is completed.

There are two reasons for this recommendation. First, by putting your agreement in writing you will not have to worry about the complex legal rules that determine whether the agreement must be written.

Second, and perhaps more importantly, you will avoid the consequences of memory failure. Even when the law allows oral contracts, the two sides to a contract will often have different recollections of the details of their negotiation and agreement. Their views might differ about when the agreement starts, how long it continues, how it can be terminated, and so on. These memory problems are avoided when you sign a written agreement. Be guided by a Chinese proverb: "Even the palest ink is better than the best memory."

Parol Evidence Rule. A separate risk arises after you reduce your agreement to writing. To illustrate this risk, assume that you have just been hired by a company in a city distant from your own. During negotiations the company promises to pay for your moving costs, but when the agreement is put into writing this promise is not included. Are you legally entitled to moving costs, assuming that the company admits it made the promise?

Although the law varies from country to country, under the law of the United States and many other countries, the Parol Evidence Rule states that once you put your agreement into writing, evidence of prior or contemporaneous agreements (such as the company's promise to pay your moving costs) cannot be used as evidence if you decide to sue the company.

This rule makes sense because when negotiating a contract both sides might make many agreements that they later cast aside and don't intend to include in the final contract. If they were allowed to bring evidence of these agreements into court, courts would forever be reviewing and attempting to untangle the details of what happened during the negotiations.

Even when you negotiate a contract under the laws of a country that has not adopted the Parol Evidence Rule, it is likely that your contract will include a provision stating that the rule applies. These provisions appear under a variety of headings—for example, merger clause, integration clause, or entire agreement clause.

It is good practice to include one of these provisions, even when negotiating in countries that have adopted the Parol Evidence Rule, because the rule might not apply in all situations. For example, as mentioned, the United States has adopted the CISG, which does not include the rule. Therefore, if you enter into a contract for the international sale of goods governed by the CISG, evidence of prior agreements might be admissible in court unless you include a merger clause clearly stating that evidence outside the written contract is not admissible.

Here is an example of a typical contract provision (from the US Securities and Exchange Commission archives). In January 2012, Facebook founder Mark Zuckerberg signed a contract amending an earlier employment agreement naming him president and chief executive officer of the company. The agreement contained the following standard provisions:

1. *Compensation.* Base wage of $500,000, along with bonus provision. (Notably, by early 2016 Zuckerberg was worth an estimated $49 billion. When the contract was signed he owned approximately 28% of Facebook stock.)

2. *Employee benefits.* Up to 21 days of paid time off per year.

3. *Confidentiality agreement.* Relates to a separate confidentiality and invention assignment agreement.

4. *No conflicting obligations.* Prohibits oral or written agreements that conflict with company policy.

5. *Outside activities.* No other business activity without the company's consent.

6. *Zuckerberg's general obligations.* Includes honesty, integrity, loyalty, and professionalism.

7. *At-will employment.* Can be fired at any time.

8. *Withholdings.* Compensation is paid after subtracting withholding payments.

The contract concluded with this sentence: "This letter agreement supercedes and replaces any prior understandings or agreements, whether oral, written or implied, between you and the Company regarding the matters described in this letter." Through this statement, Zuckerberg and Facebook have affirmed the Parol Evidence Rule.

Form of the writing. Contracts do not have to be printed in a formal document that says "Contract" at the top. Any writing will usually suffice—but this can be a trap. For example, two individuals were having some drinks at a restaurant. One of them, Lucy, offered to buy Zehmer's 472-acre farm for $50,000. Zehmer accepted the offer and wrote on a restaurant order form: "We hereby agree to sell to W.O. Lucy the Ferguson Farm complete for $50,000, title satisfactory to buyer." Zehmer and his wife signed the document.

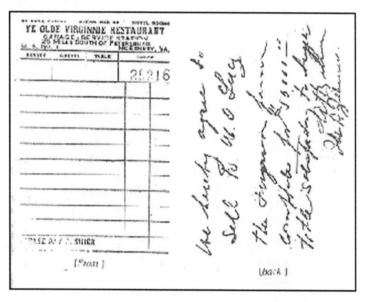

Zehmer later reneged on the agreement, claiming that he thought Lucy was kidding. He also argued that he "was as high as a Georgia pine" and that the negotiation was between "two doggoned drunks bluffing to see who could talk the biggest." In deciding that Zehmer had to give up his farm because this was a valid contract, the court emphasized several factors that indicated that this was intended to be a serious business transaction, including the appearance and completeness of the contract.[3]

Implied terms. Whether or not your agreement is written, there might be additional terms implied by the law. For example, assume that you recently moved to the United States. Some friends want you to be the catcher on their baseball team. They tell you that the pitcher on the team throws a knuckleball pitch. You have never played baseball and have no idea what that means.

A local high school baseball coach is holding a garage sale and is selling some baseball gear. You visit the sale knowing that the seller is a baseball coach and tell him that you need a catcher's mitt that will catch knuckleballs. The coach points to a mitt while stating that it is the only catcher's mitt for sale. You then negotiate a price. After buying the mitt, you discover that it is much too small to catch knuckleballs. Can you sue the coach for breach of contract?

Although you never discussed it during the negotiation, the UCC (the law governing the sale of goods) provides that in these circumstances a seller like the coach gives you an implied warranty that the item sold is fit for the particular purpose for which you need the product, in this case, catching knuckleballs. The coach is thus in breach of this implied warranty.

The Law Pillar: Contract Risk Management

Business contracts are defined as value-creating agreements enforceable by law. For example, when you enter into a contract with a supplier, you anticipate that the supplier's product will enable you to increase the value of your own products, which in turn is passed on to your customers.

Traditionally, lawyers have focused on the "enforceable by law" part of the contract definition. Their goal is to construct legally perfect, enforceable agreements that minimize legal risk. The lawyers' orientation is not surprising given their mindset. Lawyers are trained to look at contracts through the eyes of a judge who might eventually rule on a contract dispute. Thus, a good contract, from the lawyers' perspective, is one that minimizes the client's risk and is enforceable in court.

In meeting their risk management goals, lawyers focus on contract provisions designed to protect their clients. A leading international association of contract negotiators, the International Association for Contract and Commercial Management ("IACCM"), conducts an annual survey of thousands of its members (from both common law and civil law countries) to determine the contract terms that are most negotiated. Here is the 2013–14 list:

1. Limitation of Liability
2. Price/Charge/Price Changes
3. Indemnification
4. Service Levels and Warranties
5. Payment

A report on the survey results concluded that most "business-to-business negotiations are dominated by discussions over financial issues (price and payment) and risk allocation (liabilities, indemnities, data security, performance undertakings and liquidated damages)...."[4]

Limitation of liability and indemnification clauses are especially important. Limitation of liability clauses limit the damages a party to a contract can recover for actions by the other side that cause harm. Here is an example of a clause that a design professional might want to include in a contract:

> The Design Professional, and its consultants, partners, agents and employees, shall not be liable to the Owner, whether jointly, severally or individually, in excess of the compensation paid to the Design Professional under this Agreement, or in excess of the sum of $_____, whichever is greater, as a result of any act or omission not amounting to

a willful or intentional wrong.[5]

Instead of limiting liability, indemnification clauses are agreements to accept responsibility for certain acts. For example, if you license your software to a licensee, you would want to include in the contract a clause such as the following, which requires the licensee to cover you for losses resulting from using the software.

> Licensee shall hold harmless and indemnify Board, System, University, its Regents, officers, employees and agents from and against any claims, demands, or causes of action whatsoever, including without limitation those arising on account of any injury or death of persons or damage to property caused by, or arising out of, or resulting from, the exercise or practice of the license granted hereunder by Licensee, its Subsidiaries or their officers, employees, agents, or representatives.[6]

For examples of other types of risk management clauses, review the Facebook contract with Mark Zuckerberg that was summarized earlier. The eight provisions in his contract include confidentiality, inventions, conflicts of interest, outside activities, and employment at-will.

Aligning the Strategy Pillar with the Law Pillar: Reframing Contracts to Create Value

As noted in the previous section, business contracts are value-creating agreements that are enforceable by law. While "enforceable by law" is important and cannot be ignored, legal risk management must be balanced with the "value-creating agreement" part of the definition. In other words, while you want your agreements to be enforceable, you also want contracts that enable you to achieve your business goals. As law professors Ian Macneil and Paul Gudel note in their book *Contracts: Exchange Transactions and Relations* (2002), "only lawyers and other trouble-oriented folk look on contracts primarily as a source of trouble and disputation, rather than a way of getting things done."

This section explains two approaches you can use to reconcile the tension between the Strategy Pillar (with its emphasis on value creation) and Law Pillar (with its emphasis on risk management): (i) a lean contracting strategy that reshapes the content of contracts and (ii) visualization, which is designed to make legal concepts more understandable.

Simplify Your Contracts Through Lean Contracting

A lean contracting strategy might enable you to focus on creating value while minimizing legal complexity. This strategy applies lean production concepts to the "production" of contracts by asking whether company contracts can be simplified by considering the costs and benefits of various contract clauses.

For example, the in-house legal team at the brewing company Scottish & Newcastle sensed that company resources were being wasted in the contract negotiation process. Their work in developing what they call the Pathclearer approach to commercial contracting—a form of lean contracting—illustrates the potential benefits of reorienting contracting strategy. Unless otherwise noted, the quotations in this chapter regarding this approach are from a highly-recommended article by Weatherley titled "Pathclearer—A more commercial approach to drafting commercial contracts."[7]

Purpose of a contract. The Scottish & Newcastle lawyers initially asked three fundamental questions. First, what is the purpose of a contract? In answering this question, they used a traditional definition of a legal contract:

> [T]he only purpose of a contract… is to ensure that rights and obligations which the parties agree to can be enforced

in court (or arbitration). Put even more bluntly, the essence of a contract is the ability to force someone else to do something they don't want to do, or to obtain compensation for their failure.

With this definition in mind, they realized that certain terms, such as product specifications, should always be in writing and that certain types of deals, such as "share purchases, loan agreements, and guarantees," require detailed written contracts.

But they also realized that many other scenarios—for example, a long-term relationship between a customer and supplier—call for a "much lighter legal touch." They recognized that in these situations, the consequences of forcing contractual obligations on an unwilling partner through "begrudging performance" or litigation are not attractive.

They concluded that leaving long-term relationships to "free market economics [is better than an] attempt to place continuing contractual obligations on each other." In other words, freedom of the market should dominate the traditional freedom of contract philosophy that has led to detailed written contracts.

Drawbacks of traditional detailed contracts. The second of the lawyers' three fundamental questions focused on the risks associated with traditional, law-oriented contracts: "What are the drawbacks of detailed written contracts?" In answering this question, the in-house lawyers reached six insightful conclusions.

1.   *Illusory and costly attempts to reach certainty.* "The apparent certainty and protection of a detailed written contract… [are] often illusory" and wasteful as companies pay their lawyers, first for drafting contracts that only the lawyers understand, and second for interpreting what the contracts mean.

     The in-house legal team witnessed "bizarre attempts" by

lawyers attempting to reach certainty. For example, external lawyers spent "hours drafting and debating the precise legal definition of beer for insertion in a simple beer supply agreement." The legal team also recognized the futility of trying to predict the future.

2. *Dispute resolution.* Detailed contracts can result in legalistic dispute resolution. As the lawyers observed:

> Without a detailed contract, business people who become involved in a dispute will generally discuss the issue and reach a sensible agreement on how to resolve it.... However, where a detailed contract exists, the same parties will feel obliged to consult their lawyers.

This conclusion brings to mind my recent conversation with a CEO. In his opinion, the only purpose of a contract is, as he put it, to "give a right to sue." When disputes arose between his company and its customers he advised his staff to ignore the contract and work out a solution that met the customers' needs.

3. *Complexity.* The complexity of contracts causes confusion and creates a risk that the parties will be unable to focus on key terms; indeed, it becomes "difficult to see the wood for the trees."

4. *Unnecessary terms.* The general law of contracts provides "a fair middle-ground solution to most issues" and "[t]he beauty of simply relying on the 'general law,' rather than trying to set out the commercial arrangement in full in a detailed written contract, is that there is no need to negotiate the non-key terms of a deal."

5. *Expense.* Negotiating detailed written contracts is expensive

in terms of management time, lawyer time, and delayed business opportunities.

6. *Wrong focus.* Detailed written contracts can cause the parties to focus on worst-case scenarios that "can lead to the souring of relationships... [C]ontinuing business relationships are like butterflies. They are subtle and hard to capture. When you do try to nail them down, you can kill them in the process."

The lawyers might have added to this list the concerns that arise when negotiating with individuals from other cultures. For example, in countries such as China, developing a relationship with someone you trust is more important than trying to cover all contingencies in a lengthy contract.

The "wrong focus" problem (#6) is illustrated by the IACCM surveys mentioned previously. As noted earlier, the surveys conclude that the most-negotiated contract provisions relate to risk management. But none of the most-negotiated clauses are on the 2013-14 list of most important terms listed below:

1. Scope and goals
2. Responsibilities of the parties
3. Change management
4. Delivery/acceptance
5. Communications and reporting

In other words, the provisions considered most important for contract creation and enforcement receive less attention from negotiators than do less important clauses oriented toward risk management. A report on the survey results concluded that this disconnect does "not contribute to the win-win approach that negotiators claim they prefer. In past surveys, almost 80% of participants acknowledge that the focus of their negotiations do not result in the best outcome for either party."[8]

Other ways to achieve business goals. The third and final question the in-house legal team asked is whether negotiators can achieve their business goals without detailed written contracts. The Scottish & Newcastle lawyers answered this question affirmatively by focusing on the concept of "commercial affinity."

Commercial affinity is the force that keeps parties together in "mutually beneficial commercial relationships." Aligning the parties' interests through carefully-constructed incentives, combined with the right of either side to walk away from the deal if it ceases to be attractive economically, incentivizes them to meet the other side's needs and alleviates the need for "a myriad of tactical rights and obligations in a contract."

In summary, the Scottish & Newcastle lawyers realized that a different approach is appropriate "when the parties are in a continuing business relationship, rather than just carrying out a snapshot transaction" that might require a detailed written contract. They do not advocate, however, a complete return to handshake agreements. For example, "exit arrangements (such as obligations to buy dedicated assets from the supplier...) do need to be spelled out in the contract." By focusing on the three fundamental questions, they realized that in many other situations leaner contracts were possible.

A lean contract that the company negotiated with a service provider illustrates the company's Pathclearer approach in a continuing business relationship. The two parties initially had a ten-year contract that consumed more than 200 pages. During contract renegotiations, they used the Pathclearer approach to reduce the size of the contract significantly by giving each party termination rights after twelve months' notice—in essence, a mutual "nuclear button."

> By giving ourselves the ability to terminate at any time, we avoided the need to have to negotiate detailed terms in

the contract…. This is a much more powerful way of influencing the service provider than a technical debate over whether they were complying with the words set out in the contract.

The following figure illustrates a contract between a US beer company (Coors) and one of its bottle suppliers—twenty-three pages plus eight pages of exhibits.

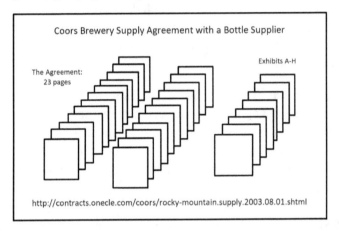

Contrast the Coors contract with a Scottish & Newcastle Pathclearer contract with one of its bottle suppliers—one page plus one attachment.

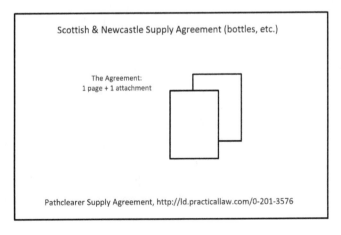

Use Visualization to Understand Your Negotiations and Contracts

As the contract diagrams illustrate, a picture can be worth a thousand words. Using pictures and other forms of visualization can help you clarify your negotiation decisions and better understand the terms of the contract you are negotiating.

Visualizing negotiation decisions. In making your contracts leaner, you might be able to eliminate or soften certain provisions that cause expensive contract negotiations. Visualization can help you identify these provisions.

For example, an indemnity clause in Microsoft's contracts caused many contract negotiations to last an additional sixty to ninety days, because customers did not want to provide the indemnity Microsoft requested. Microsoft softened the provision after realizing that the benefits of the clause were minimal in contrast to potential costs such as reputational costs (resulting from confrontational negotiations), resource costs (managers' and lawyers' time), and cash flow costs (from delayed sales during the additional two to three months of contract negotiation).

In describing and commenting on these costs, Tim Cummins, CEO of IACCM, concluded that "risk management is about balancing consequence and probability. Here is an example where consequence was managed without regard to probability—and as a result, other risks and exposures [such as reputational and resource costs] became inevitable."[9]

Decision trees are useful in visualizing negotiation decisions that balance risk and probability, like Microsoft faced. Let's assume that the contract clause in question provided Microsoft with $20 million in indemnity, and there is a 1% chance that the company will lose $20 million and invoke the clause. (This probability can be estimated on the basis of your company's past experience. In practice, the chance that such a clause would be invoked is probably less than 1%.)

Let's also assume that management and lawyer time to negotiate the indemnity and cash flow costs resulting from delayed sales during negotiations total $1 million. In effect, Microsoft would pay $1 million for the equivalent of a $20 million insurance policy. Given these assumptions, should Microsoft pay $1 million for this insurance?

The following decision tree depicts the 1% chance that Microsoft will lose $20 million if it drops the indemnification clause demand and the 99% chance that it will lose nothing. This results in an expected value of –$200,000 (0.99 × 0 + 0.01 × $20 million). Based on these assumed values and probabilities (and not factoring in its attitude toward risk), Microsoft made a wise decision when it softened its negotiating stance.

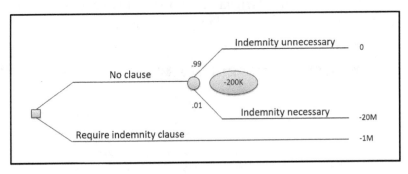

In this case, we assumed that Microsoft's negotiation costs were $1 million. Sometimes the lost opportunities relating to slow negotiations are much higher. For example, a prominent oil and gas attorney told me that he represented a company that negotiated the sale of property to a buyer for $30 million. Signing the contract was delayed when the buyer's law firm insisted on a clause that immunized the buyer from a low-probability event. As negotiations regarding this clause were in process, another buyer offered to pay more than $100 million for the property. The law firm's desire for a perfect legal contract cost the client more than $70 million!

Visualizing contract provisions and other legal documents. Visualization can also help you understand the terms in a contract and in other legally complex documents. For example, contracts are often filled with clauses such as the following, which challenge the cognitive skills of negotiators:

> This Agreement shall be valid for an initial period of three (3) years from the date of signing. Unless either Party gives notice of termination at least six (6) months before the expiry of the three-year period, it shall remain in force until further notice, with a notice period of at least three (3) months. Notice shall be given in writing.[10]

In the following diagram, leaders in the visualization movement Stefania Passera and Helena Haapio (my frequent co-author) show how visualization can clarify the meaning of this clause.

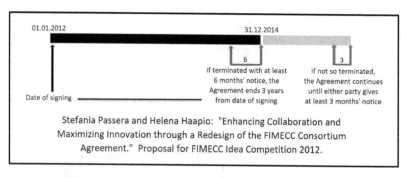

Stefania Passera and Helena Haapio: "Enhancing Collaboration and Maximizing Innovation through a Redesign of the FIMECC Consortium Agreement." Proposal for FIMECC Idea Competition 2012.

Another example illustrates the value of using visualization when dealing with other forms of complex legal documents. In 2013, Helena Haapio invited me to a Legal Design Jam, a design hackathon to visualize the Wikimedia Foundation's trademark policy. She was a facilitator, along with Stefania Passera, Margaret Hagen from Stanford, and Yana Welinder, Legal Counsel for the Foundation. The small group of participants included a mixture of designers and attorneys.

Before the redesign effort, the trademark policy was a typical densely-worded legal document. The end result of the Legal Design Jam was a revised policy that is colorful and clear: http://wikimediafoundation.org/wiki/Trademark_policy.

At this website, a green checkmark is used to denote situations in which users can freely use marks, such as when they are used to discuss Wikimedia sites in literary works. An orange question mark is used in situations where permission is required (such as when you want "to use the Wikipedia logo in a movie"), and a red "x" indicates uses that are prohibited (for example, when you create a website that mimics a Wikimedia site).

Key Takeaways

Successful contracts are the key to business success; without them no business can survive. Contracting, perhaps more than any other business activity, creates tension between the Law Pillar's emphasis on risk management and the Strategy Pillar's focus on value creation. To bridge the gap between these pillars you should:

1. **Become legally savvy about contract law.** Understand the sources of contract law and the four-part checklist that provides a framework for your contract negotiations.

2. **Manage your contracting risks.** Decide whether to include provisions in your contracts that are designed to protect your interests, notably indemnification and limitation of liability.

3. **Focus on creating value during the contracting process.** Consider lean contracting possibilities as a means to focus on the business elements in your contracts. Using visualization will help you clarify understanding of your contracts.

7 Use Dispute Resolution Processes for Value Creation

Like the contracting process (Chapter 6), dispute resolution processes—especially litigation—play an important role in business success because they affect all stakeholders. These processes usually are associated with risk management and minimizing liability. However, as we will see in this chapter, these processes also have the potential to create value.

Legal Briefing on Dispute Resolution

This briefing focuses on alternatives to litigation that are designed to keep you out of court. As noted in Chapter 1, these alternatives fall under the collective heading of "alternative dispute resolution" ("ADR").

Understanding ADR processes is important for at least three reasons. First, during your business negotiations you must decide whether to include ADR provisions in your contracts. To understand what you are negotiating, you should understand the basics of the two key ADR processes: mediation and arbitration.

Even when your attorney is involved in the negotiations, you might have to take the lead in negotiating ADR clauses. According to one study, around one-third of attorneys "never advised their clients to try mediation or arbitration."[1] This is what legendary litigator Joe Jamail had to say about mediation: "I'm a trial lawyer.... There are some lawyers who do nothing but this mediation bull****. Do you know what the root of mediation is? Mediocrity!"[2]

On the other hand, many lawyers are enthusiastic about ADR. Perhaps Gandhi said it best:

> My joy was boundless. I had learned the true practice of law. I had learned to find out the better side of human nature and to enter men's hearts. I realized that the true function of a lawyer was to unite parties.... The lesson was so indelibly burnt into me that a large part of my time during the last 20 years of my practice as a lawyer was occupied in bringing about private compromises of hundreds of cases. I lost nothing thereby—not even money, certainly not my soul.[3]

The second reason why understanding ADR processes is important is that you might participate in these processes if you are involved in a business dispute. If you have agreed to arbitration, for example, you will participate in selecting the arbitrator, you must decide whether you need an attorney, you should understand whether you can appeal the arbitrator's decision, and so on.

Third, in the course of your business life and personal life, you might play the role of a third party as you resolve work disputes or family disputes. At a minimum, you should be able to make an informed decision about whether it is better to act as an arbitrator or whether a mediator role makes more sense.

This section opens by describing a process that is often considered the enemy of business—litigation. "Alternative" in alternative dispute resolution refers to alternatives to litigation, which is viewed as an expensive and time-consuming process. To understand when and how to use ADR, you should first understand litigation. We will then turn to the two key ADR processes—arbitration and mediation.

Litigation

There are fundamental differences between litigation in the United States and other countries. In a global economy, it is especially important for you to understand these differences so that you can make sound decisions regarding litigation strategy and settlement possibilities. Here are five key differences.

1. **Contingency fees.** In the United States, lawyers can be hired on a contingency fee basis, which means that their fees are contingent on the outcome of the case. For example, if a lawyer hired on a 30% contingency fee basis wins $10 million, the fee would be $3 million. If the lawyer loses the case, the fee would be 30% of zero. In recent years the contingency fee system has spread to several countries beyond the United States.

2. **Punitive damages.** In countries around the world, the purpose of damages is to compensate a party injured by someone else. In certain circumstances, courts in the United States will also award punitive damages designed to punish someone whose actions were intentional, malicious, or reckless.

3. **Discovery.** Discovery is the process by which lawyers uncover evidence that is used in litigation. US courts have historically been more liberal than elsewhere in allowing lawyers to search for evidence by rummaging through documents the opposing party holds.

4. **Juries.** In the United States, unlike most countries, juries are allowed to decide civil cases.

5. **"American Rule."** In the United States the traditional rule is that each side must pay its own attorney's fees, even the party that wins the case. Other countries have a "Loser

Pays" rule (also known as the "Everywhere but America Rule"), where the losing party must pay the winner's legal fees.

In combination, these features of the US system can make litigation an attractive process for plaintiffs. For example, if I hire an attorney on a contingency fee basis to sue you, you would hire your own attorney to defend the case. If the court dismisses the lawsuit, I would owe my attorney nothing because the fee would be contingent on a successful outcome. And under the American Rule, I would not have to cover your attorney fees even though I am the losing party.

A Case Example. To illustrate the US system, let's examine a case decided by the Tennessee Supreme Court, 2008, *Flax v. DaimlerChrysler*. In this case, a grandfather drove a Dodge Caravan with three passengers—a friend who was sitting in the front seat, the driver's daughter in the seat behind her father, and his eight-month-old grandson in the seat behind the passenger. Someone driving a pickup truck well over the speed limit crashed into the rear end of the Caravan, causing the passenger's seatback to collapse onto the baby, who died from his injuries.

Although not discussed in the case, we can assume that negotiations between the car company and the parents over damages were unsuccessful. We can also assume that the parents hired an attorney on a **contingency fee** basis, although this was not discussed in the case.

Cases begin with filing a complaint. In their complaint, the baby's parents alleged that the seats were defective and that the company failed to warn consumers. In answering the complaint, the company denied that the seats were defective.

The next stage after the complaint and answer is **discovery**. In this case, the parents' attorney discovered that the company's Safety

183

Leadership Team had concluded "that the seats were inadequate to protect consumers." The company had ordered the minutes destroyed from a meeting where this issue was discussed, disbanded the team, and fired the team chair.

The next stage is the trial, where a **jury** awarded the parents $5 million in damages for the wrongful death of their baby and another $98 million in **punitive damages**. The trial and appellate courts eventually reduced the punitive damages to $13.4 million, so the damages ultimately totaled $18.4 million. Although not discussed by the court, we can assume that under the **American Rule**, the parents' attorney fees were deducted from this total and were not recoverable from the company.

One feature that the US system unfortunately shares with other legal systems is that the process takes a long time. The accident in this case took place on June 30, 2001; the final decision in the case was reached almost eight years later on May 26, 2009.

Psychological Damage of Litigation. In his article "Litigation as Violence," Vincent Cardi notes that being involved in litigation can cause psychological damage that includes symptoms such as "stress, anxiety, depression, irritability, difficulties in concentration, loss of motivation, loss of social involvement, loss of enjoyment and pleasure in life, aches and pains, low self-esteem...."

As if these aren't enough, personal injury litigation such as product liability (see Chapter 2) can produce these additional symptoms:

> insomnia, tension, restlessness, dizziness, appetite disturbances, low energy, lowered self-esteem problems, disruptions of attention and concentration, indecisiveness, agitation, feelings of hopelessness and pessimism, disruptions of sexual functioning, distressing dreams, headaches, numerous other physical complaints, and related problems affecting marriage and family life.[4]

Clearly, ADR makes sense in terms of maintaining your health in addition to the potential time and cost savings.

Although these symptoms accentuate the value of alternative processes, the litigation process is not devoid of humor. Here, for a bit of levity, is a list of questions lawyers have asked. They were collected by the editor of the *Massachusetts Bar Association Lawyer's Journal* from unverified newspaper accounts:[5]

- "Now doctor, isn't it true that when a person dies in his sleep he doesn't know about it until the next morning?"
- "Were you present when your picture was taken?"
- "Were you alone or by yourself?"
- "Was it you or your younger brother who was killed in the war?"
- "Did he kill you?"
- "The youngest son, the 20-year-old, how old is he?"
- "How far apart were the vehicles at the time of the collision?"
- "How many times have you committed suicide?"

We now turn to the two primary alternatives to litigation—arbitration and mediation. Like the litigation process (which involves a judge) both processes use so-called third parties: an arbitrator and a mediator.

Arbitration

Agreements to resolve disputes through arbitration permeate our personal lives. If you use a credit card, have automobile insurance, buy stock, use eBay, or use Amazon, you probably have agreed to arbitrate your disputes. For example, my (and your) arbitration agreement with Amazon provides:

> Any dispute or claim relating in any way to your use of any Amazon Service, or to any products or services sold

> or distributed by Amazon or through Amazon.com will be resolved by binding arbitration, rather than in court.... There is no judge or jury in arbitration, and court review of an arbitration award is limited.

Beyond consumer agreements, arbitration is a common business dispute resolution process and is even used to resolve disputes with governments. In 2014, an international arbitration tribunal decided that Russia owes $50 billion to the shareholders of Yukos as compensation for company assets that were seized.[6]

The Arbitration Process. The arbitration process generally follows this sequence, as noted in *A Guide to Mediation and Arbitration for Business People.*[7]

Agreement. In most situations arbitration is not used unless you first agree to the process. You can agree when you first enter into a contract, as in the Amazon example, or you can agree after a dispute arises.

Selecting an arbitrator. Your agreement might provide that an arbitration service, such as the American Arbitration Association, will provide a list of potential arbitrators from a roster it maintains. If you and the other side cannot agree on an arbitrator from the list, the service can name one for you.

You can also use a more informal approach when selecting an arbitrator. For example, if you are creating a partnership with another person, you could provide in your agreement that if a dispute arises each of you will appoint an arbitrator and these two arbitrators will then select a third arbitrator.

Hearing and award. The arbitration hearing is much like a trial in court, and you must decide whether to be represented by an attorney. The arbitrator has the power to subpoena witnesses if necessary. The hearing will begin with an opening statement, followed by an examination and cross-examination of witnesses, as well as a closing statement.

Unlike litigation, the hearing is private and the arbitrator will normally use common sense rather than technical rules of court procedure in deciding what evidence is relevant to the case.

Following the hearing, the arbitrator will reach a decision. Although not always the case, the arbitrator might make the decision without providing an opinion that explains the rationale for the decision. If the losing party does not comply with the award, the decision can be enforced by a court.

Appeals. Because public policy favors the finality of arbitration awards, the ability to appeal an award using the court system is limited. Although courts might overturn an award when, for example, the arbitrator is engaged in corruption or fraud, they will not usually intervene even when the arbitrator makes a mistake regarding the facts or the law.

This rule of finality was cited in a California case.[8] A City of Palo Alto employee threatened other employees with physical violence and even threatened to shoot them. The employees treated the threats as jokes. The employee also said that he could kill someone while 600 yards away. He owned eighteen rifles and pistols and had a personalized license plate that read "SHOOOT."

Following a dispute, the employee in question threatened to shoot another employee, that employee's wife, and his baby. This led to an arrest for making a terrorist threat, and he eventually pled guilty to disturbing the peace. The City also obtained an injunction that prohibited the employee from having any contact with the person he threatened and decided to terminate his employment.

The City's decision then went to an arbitrator as allowed under a union contract. The arbitrator decided, among other things, that the threats were "everyday 'boy talk'" that were tolerated at this workplace and were not genuine. As a result, the arbitrator ordered reinstatement of the employee to his position and awarded him back pay.

On appeal, the court quoted precedent that "judicial review of arbitration awards is extremely narrow" and that "an arbitrator's decision is not generally reviewable for errors of fact or law [even when it] causes substantial injustice to the parties." In an unusual twist in this case, however, the court eventually decided that the employee could not be reinstated because of the earlier injunction.

If you want to use arbitration but are concerned about placing too much power in the hands of an arbitrator whose decision usually will not be reviewed by courts, you can try to negotiate an arbitration agreement that includes an appeals process. For example, effective November 2013, the American Arbitration Association adopted rules permitting an appeal to a panel of arbitrators that can review "errors of law that are material and prejudicial, and determinations of fact that are clearly erroneous."[9]

The Costs of Arbitration. Negotiators often attempt to include arbitration agreements in contracts because of perceived cost savings. But certain aspects of arbitration might be more expensive than litigation. Based on cost estimates from experts in Texas, Florida, and Pennsylvania, the arbitration of a $600,000 construction dispute would cost $25,400 for the filing fee, case service, and compensation for the arbitrator. The comparable litigation cost would total $300 for a filing fee (because the case service, judge, and courtroom are free).

The total litigation costs, however, would be $120,300 compared to $94,500 for arbitration. One reason for this is that legal fees for litigation are much higher than those for arbitration. Legal fees for preparing for and attending the trial alone are $12,000 higher than for attending an arbitration hearing. And an appeal of the court decision would add substantially to the cost differential.[10]

Mediation

Mediation is the second of the two basic ADR processes. In essence, mediation is a negotiation assisted by a third party. Traditionally, the goal of mediation was to solve a specific problem using one of two mediation processes. In the first process, facilitative mediation, the mediator's role is to make it easier for the parties to discuss and resolve their concerns. In the second process, evaluative mediation, the mediator is also asked to evaluate the merits of each side's case without making a decision (unlike arbitration).

In recent years, a third option has developed—transformative mediation. Although transformative mediation might also result in solving a specific problem, the ultimate goal is to improve the relationship between the parties. After the US Postal Service adopted transformative mediation in the 1990s, it saved millions of dollars in legal costs and productivity improvements.[11]

I once asked someone who had researched mediation at the Postal Service for an example of transformation mediation. She mentioned a letter carrier who had filed a sexual harassment claim against her supervisor. Through transformative mediation, the parties discovered that the real problem was their relationship. The supervisor referred to the letter carrier and other letter carriers by their route numbers; the postal worker felt that this was dehumanizing. After the relationship was fixed and the supervisor started referring to the letter carrier personally, the complaint was withdrawn.

The Caucus. One especially effective tool many mediators use is the caucus. With a caucus, the mediator meets separately with each side to discuss their interests and positions. The mediator keeps each set of information confidential if the parties so desire. With this confidential information in mind, the mediator can either help the parties reach an agreement or advise them that the mediation is a waste of time.

Be Creative in Using ADR Processes

The two basic models of dispute resolution—arbitration and mediation—provide many opportunities for creativity and innovation. In one case at the outer limits of creativity, a judge, apparently fed up with the parties' relying on the federal courts, decided to "fashion a new form of alternative dispute resolution, to wit: at 4:00 p.m. on Friday, June 30, 2006, counsel shall convene at a neutral site…[and] shall engage in one game of 'rock, paper, scissors' to determine who wins a motion."[12]

The mini-trial and rent-a-judge are two prominent examples of mediation and arbitration variations.

Mini-Trial. The mini-trial is a variation of the mediation model. The prototypical mini-trial involved a $6 million intellectual property lawsuit filed by Telecredit against TRW. This lawsuit began much like any other. The parties spent around $500,000 and exchanged 100,000 documents, with no resolution in sight. Given the slow pace of the litigation, executives from the two companies created a structured process that came to be known as a mini-trial.

The process essentially involved five parties: one attorney and one executive from each side and a neutral expert on intellectual property. The attorneys each had a half day to explain their respective versions of the case and to answer questions from the executives. The executives then met briefly and resolved the case.

The estimated savings in legal fees was around $1 million. Through this process, the executives were able to hear the case as presented by the other side's attorney (which might have been quite different from what they heard up to that point from their own attorneys). They were also able to resolve the case in a way that made business sense, as opposed to a typical court decision that produces a zero sum result (in this case with one side winning and the other side losing $6 million).

Rent-a-Judge. Rent-a-judge, a variation of the arbitration model, uses retired judges as arbitrators. Although the hearing is similar to a trial, rent-a-judge offers the same benefits as other forms of arbitration. When Brad Pitt and Jennifer Anniston used rent-a-judge to handle their divorce in 2005, they were able to select their own judge (presumably a judge who was familiar with divorce proceedings). They were also able to conclude the divorce proceeding quickly and maintain their privacy because the press was not allowed to attend the hearing.[13]

The Law Pillar: Dispute Resolution and Risk Management

Risk management begins with understanding the two key third-party processes—arbitration and mediation—that are alternatives to litigation. To use them effectively, however, four key ADR tools are recommended for managing risks relating to business disputes: a corporate pledge, screens, contract clauses, and online resources.

Corporate Pledge

The International Institute for Conflict Prevention & Resolution ("CPR") was a pioneer in developing a pledge that companies can adopt as a statement of their corporate policy. The key sentence in the pledge states: "In the event of a business dispute between our company and another company, which has made or will then make a similar statement, we are prepared to explore with that other party resolution of the dispute through negotiation or ADR techniques before pursuing full-scale litigation." More than 4,000 operating companies have adopted this policy.[14]

Suitability Screens

Suitability screens are a series of questions designed to help parties select a binding or non-binding form of dispute resolution. Binding processes are arbitration and litigation; non-binding processes are mediation and negotiation.

CPR publishes an especially useful *ADR Suitability Guide* that features a mediation screen. In helping the disputing parties decide whether to use mediation, the screen asks questions that focus on the following factors, among others:

- The parties' relationship
- Importance of control over the process and decision
- Importance of discovery
- Chances for success in court
- Cost of litigation
- Importance of speed and privacy
- Relative power of both sides

Contract Clauses

Parties can enter into an ADR contract as part of the initial business negotiation before a dispute arises or they can wait until after a dispute develops. Post-dispute agreements are often difficult to negotiate because the relationship of the parties has soured. Here is an example of a pre-dispute agreement, which is part of Oracle's letter offering Mark Hurd the position of president:

> You and Oracle understand and agree that any existing or future dispute or claim arising out of or related to your Oracle employment, or the termination of that employment, will be resolved by final and binding arbitration and that no other forum for dispute resolution will be available to either party, except as to those claims identified below. The decision of the arbitrator shall be final and binding on both you and Oracle and it shall be enforceable by any court having proper jurisdiction.[15]

ADR contract clauses might provide for only one process, such as Mark Hurd's arbitration clause, or the processes can be linked. For example, the parties might agree to use negotiation and/or mediation before turning to arbitration.

Online Dispute Resolution

In recent years advances in technology have enabled ADR to become online dispute resolution ("ODR"). Online systems allow parties to use negotiation, mediation, and arbitration to resolve business and personal disputes.

Your decision to use online dispute resolution involves a cost–benefit analysis. On the one hand, online processes save travel costs and are convenient. On the other hand, there is evidence that they are less effective—especially because it is difficult to build a relationship with the opposing side. One way to surmount this problem is to combine face-to-face negotiation with online ODR by scheduling face time at the outset of the negotiation before moving to the online phase.

Align the Strategy Pillar with the Law Pillar by Reframing ADR to Create Value

Linking dispute resolution to value creation is especially difficult for many business leaders who view litigation and other processes as a waste of time and money. Because of this difficulty, those who can bridge the gap between the Strategy Pillar and Law Pillar have an opportunity to create *sustainable* competitive advantage. This section reviews three value-creating opportunities: dispute prevention, using ADR for deal making, and using litigation to create value.

Dispute Prevention

Often overlooked by business leaders and lawyers intent on

developing alternatives to litigation is the simple fact that disputes that never arise don't have to be resolved. Dispute prevention focuses on predicting what people will do rather than on what courts might decide.[16] One rationale for this principle was painfully stated by the French philosopher Voltaire: "I was never ruined but twice: once when I lost a lawsuit and once when I won one."

I had first-hand experience with dispute prevention several years ago after spending a night at a Marriott hotel in Texas. I was scheduled to give a legal briefing to a group of corporate executives the following morning and asked the front desk for a wake-up call. The call never came.

When checking out, I mentioned the missing call when completing a feedback card. A couple of weeks later, the President of Marriott, Bill Marriott, sent a personal note to my home in Stanford, California, where I was teaching at the time. In the note, he apologized for the missed call and mentioned that he had asked the hotel general manager to investigate the matter.

Another hotel adopted a different approach following a well-publicized, tragic incident. International recording star Connie Francis was raped by an intruder while staying at a Howard Johnson Motor Lodge. Her reaction: "I never received so much as a note from Mr. Howard B. Johnson saying 'We're sorry it happened.' After being shocked, I was very angry."[17] After becoming angry, she sued the hotel and eventually won $2.5 million.

We can only speculate why the hotel never communicated with Connie Francis. Probably the company leaders followed the traditional approach by asking their lawyers whether a court might hold them liable—focusing on what a court might do. The attorneys might have responded that the hotel should not be held liable for the acts of an independent third party (the rapist), and they might have gone further by advising company management not to contact the singer or do anything else that might indicate that it was liable. This was the traditional approach, which is in sharp contrast to the Marriott apology.

The two examples illustrate situations where hotels did (Marriott) and did not (Howard Johnson) use a dispute prevention approach *after* a problem occurred. You can also incorporate a preventive approach into your contracts before incidents arise. For example, a process called "partnering" is used in the construction industry. While there are many variations, this is the usual format, as described in *The Construction Industry's Guide to Dispute Avoidance and Resolution* published by the American Arbitration Association:[18]

> [R]epresentatives of the project's stakeholders attend pre-construction workshops in order to get to know each other and share concerns. Neutral facilitators guide discussions about the project, specific individual goals and agendas. It is during these meetings that participants develop ways to recognize risks that may create obstacles to the success of the project. They develop methods to avoid, control or cope with potential sources of conflict. The eventual outcome is a joint agreement signed by the workshop participants that sets forth their goals and expresses their commitment to the project.

As the hotel examples illustrate, an apology is a powerful tool for preventing and resolving disputes while creating value for a business in the form of customer retention. But the value creation aspects of an apology can also influence operations. For example, the University of Michigan Health System developed a claims management model that includes apologies (combined with compensation) to patients who receive unreasonable care.

By openly acknowledging errors, the health system is able to use patient experiences to improve processes. This model has resulted in a significant drop in lawsuits coupled with a reduction in new claims as processes have improved. As noted by the director of the Michigan model, "the real goal is to improve patient safety."[19]

Use ADR for Deal-Making

Historically, processes like arbitration and mediation have been used as alternatives to litigation for resolving disputes. In recent years, however, these processes have also been used increasingly to negotiate value-creating deals. Mediation is especially promising because the use of a caucus enables mediators to prepare a negotiation analysis that takes into account confidential information from each side.

According to one study, close to 40% of the mediators surveyed had used mediation for deals ranging from $100,000 to $26 million. Examples of the deals included negotiations involving angel investments, physician partnerships, the sale of cable television rights, and a software joint venture.[20]

Arbitration is also a possibility for resolving difficult issues during negotiations. Baseball arbitration is a highly-publicized example that is used when players are involved in salary disputes with their teams. The unique feature of baseball arbitration is that each side submits a final figure to the arbitrator, who then must select one of the two figures.

For example, assume that a deadlock arises during negotiations in which Pitcher demands a salary of $20 million and Team offers $10 million. If they use the baseball form of arbitration, Pitcher and Team would privately submit salary figures to the arbitrator, who must select one of the two numbers. Wanting the arbitrator to select their number, each side is likely to be more reasonable than when making the original demands. While commonly used to facilitate baseball negotiations, this form of arbitration could be used in any type of deal-making negotiation.

In addition to using dispute resolution processes to make a deal, you can use a dispute resolution mindset to convert a dispute into a deal that creates value for both sides. For example, I give my students a real-world scenario involving a dispute between a company that developed a statistical software package and its licensee. The company learned that the licensee was working on an adaptation of the software, which the licensee planned to market to other companies in violation of the licensing agreement. The company sued the licensee for several million dollars.

Students are given a role as leader in the company, and they must decide whether to accept a settlement offer from the licensee. Most students become adversarial and recommend against settling the lawsuit. But a few students recognize that both sides might benefit by working together to form a joint venture. Rather than letting a court determine who wins and who loses, which is a zero sum game, both sides have a chance to win through a strategic marketing plan that increases total profits that exceed the sum of their separate profits.

Use Litigation for Value Creation

Despite the risk of psychological injury discussed earlier in this chapter, litigation has value-creating opportunities for both plaintiffs and defendants. From the plaintiff's perspective, companies use so-called "plaintiff's recovery" lawsuits to turn their law departments into a source of revenue. For example, Ford Motor Company has expanded its "Affirmative Recovery" program from the United States to Europe and Asia. Switzerland-based Tyco has started an "Asset Recovery" program that focuses on recovering debts from suppliers and others. In short, in the words of a *Wall Street Journal* article, "Companies are warming to a new way of generating revenue: suing for it."[21]

From a defendant's perspective, the litigation process can generate information that is difficult for an organization to obtain elsewhere. This information comes in the form of complaints filed by plaintiffs, documents unearthed during discovery, depositions of company personnel, expert witness reports, and so on. In her article "Introspection Through Litigation," Joanna Schwartz notes that "This information, placed in the hands of an organization's leaders as the result of litigation, can be used to improve systems and personnel." She uses the example of hospitals that "analyze information from every stage of litigation to help understand weaknesses and improve the quality of care."[22]

Even an adverse conclusion to the litigation process can produce positive benefits. For example, after Home Depot settled a sex discrimination class action, the company "used the lesson of the lawsuit settlement as a springboard to develop an automated personnel hiring information system. The legally motivated system uncovered significant underutilization of employee talent and increased employee diversity, retention, and morale."[23]

Key Takeaways

Dispute resolution processes are important to business success because they touch all stakeholders. Using these processes provides an opportunity to preserve business relationships and create value. To succeed at this form of value creation you must:

1. **Become legally savvy about the menu of dispute resolution processes.** The key third party processes are litigation, arbitration, and mediation.

2. **Use risk management tools when resolving disputes.** These tools are: a corporate pledge, suitability screens, contract clauses, and online resources.

3. **Create value while resolving disputes.** Value-creating opportunities arise from preventing disputes, using ADR for deal making, and analyzing litigation for insights about how to improve your business.

IV DEVELOP VALUES WHILE CREATING VALUE

8. Create and Lead an Ethical Business

8 Create and Lead an Ethical Business

To this point, this book has focused on how you can become legally savvy so that you can manage legal risks and create value by closing the gap between the Strategy Pillar and the Law Pillar. In this final chapter, we complete the Three Pillar model by examining the Ethics Pillar of business decision making. This chapter addresses the following key questions that every business leader—ranging from the owner of a startup business to the leader of a multinational company—must address:

- How does the law influence ethical decision making within your company?
- What elements should your company include in its compliance program and code of conduct?
- How can you become an ethical leader in your business?
- Can your business meet societal needs while also creating value for shareholders?

Before moving to the first of these questions, a big picture perspective of business ethics programs is useful. According to Harvard Professor Lynn Paine and coauthor Christopher Bruner, companies use two types of programs when focusing on the Ethics Pillar: compliance programs and values programs. Compliance programs have a risk management orientation and emphasize meeting legal requirements to avoid liability. Values programs encourage ethical decision-making even when it is not legally required.

The most effective programs blend both compliance and values elements. Paine and Bruner described the danger of relying on only one element: "Just as exclusive emphasis on compliance may result in a myopic focus on 'obeying the letter of the law,' vague statements of principles, without translation into concrete standards that are consistently enforced, may leave employees with little sense of what is expected...."[1] This chapter covers the key elements that you should include in your company's compliance program as well as the values that your company should emphasize in its code of conduct.

The Law's Influence on Ethical Decision Making

The law influences ethical decision making in two ways. First, certain laws require companies to adopt programs designed to promote compliance with the law. Second, legal principles can provide guidance to managers faced with ethical dilemmas.

Laws Requiring Compliance Programs

Several US laws require businesses to adopt compliance programs.[2] Some of these laws are included in legislation—for instance the USA Patriot Act, which requires financial institutions to create programs to prevent money laundering. Other laws are embedded in regulations that government agencies develop. The Securities and Exchange Commission, for example, requires investment advisers and investment companies to adopt compliance programs designed to prevent violations of securities law.

Courts have also addressed the duty of company leaders to establish compliance programs. A key 1996 decision[3] involved healthcare company Caremark International. After the company pleaded guilty to mail fraud and paid about $250 million in damages, shareholders initiated a lawsuit claiming that individual members of the company's board of directors should pay for the losses. Although the Delaware Chancery Court approved a settlement of the lawsuit, it also noted that in some circumstances directors could be held liable for losses when they do not make a good faith attempt to ensure that the company has an adequate information and reporting system.

Even when companies are not technically required to do so by law, they have other incentives to adopt compliance programs. The US Organizational Sentencing Guidelines are especially important. The latest version of these guidelines provides that companies that have an "effective program to prevent and detect violations of law" are eligible for reduced fines following a criminal conviction.[4]

For example, assume that a company convicted of fraud for overcharging its customers paid restitution to its victims. Under the Sentencing Guidelines, the company would face a fine as low as $685,000 or as high as $54,800,000, depending on the quality of its compliance program and other Sentencing Guidelines that judges consider.[5] These guidelines are especially important because they provide a model that companies can use worldwide, even when not subject to US law. Later in this chapter, we will review a checklist of the guidelines.

Another incentive for companies to adopt compliance programs arises from rules that private organizations adopt. For example, to be listed on the New York Stock Exchange, companies must adopt a code of conduct that includes complying with the law.

Law-Based Ethical Standards

Often you can resolve an ethical dilemma by basing your decisions on legal principles. Legal rules relating to fraud, fiduciary duty, and unconscionability provide especially useful guidelines.[6] These principles frequently come into play during business negotiations.

Fraud. Fraud is defined as a false representation of a material fact that is relied on by the other side. In other words, it is illegal to lie about facts that the other side relies on during business transactions.

The false representation must relate to a fact that goes beyond puffery, the subjective boasting that is common in advertising. For example, a group of consumers sued cyclist Lance Armstrong arguing that he committed fraud by claiming that certain energy products were his "secret weapon" leading to his success. They claimed that he lied, because his real secret weapon was doping. A Los Angeles judge dismissed the case in 2014 after concluding that Armstrong's statements were puffery.[7]

Sometimes even statements that are technically true can be considered fraudulent if they need clarification. For example, a couple in Washington was interested in purchasing a hotel. During negotiations the owner gave them information about the monthly income they could make from the hotel.

After the couple completed the purchase, they learned that the hotel was being run as a house of prostitution and the monthly income the seller had mentioned was based on this activity. When they sued the seller, the court allowed them to recover damages, noting that: "A representation literally true is actionable if used to create an impression substantially false. In the case at bar there was no misrepresentation as to the amount of the income... [The owner] deceived them to their damage by failing to reveal the source of the income."[8]

Fiduciary Duty. A fiduciary duty is the highest duty of trust and loyalty, the type of duty that agents (including employees) owe their principals. Suppose, for example, that a real estate developer hires you to obtain a $10 million loan commitment from a financial institution. The developer promises you a commission of $50,000. You successfully obtain the commitment and the financial institution is so pleased with the deal that it pays you a finder's fee.

If the developer refuses to pay, are you entitled to the $50,000 commission? No, said a Georgia court.[9] The agent in that case violated the fiduciary duty owed to the developer by accepting the finder's fee. An agent cannot "compromise himself by attempting to serve two masters having a contrary interest...." In this situation, the agent should have disclosed the dual agency to both principals.

Unconscionability. Unconscionability is one of the most awkward words in the English language; when you type it, you will receive a flag for misspelling. However, it is an important concept in business negotiations when there is a power imbalance between the parties. In essence, the law requires you to act morally when you are the more powerful party.

Courts focus on two issues in deciding whether a contract is unconscionable. First, they look at the negotiation process (procedural unconscionability): Was the weaker party forced to accept the contract terms because of unequal bargaining power? Second, they look at the substance of the deal (substantive unconscionability): Are the terms of the deal so unreasonable that they violate principles of good conscience?

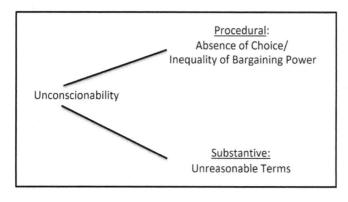

An example of unconscionability involved the restaurant Hooters, which forced employees to sign an "Agreement to arbitrate employment-related disputes." This agreement required them to arbitrate all employment disputes, including sexual harassment claims. A bartender at Hooters who signed the agreement filed suit in federal court claiming sexual harassment.

When Hooters argued that she had to use arbitration instead of going to court, the trial court concluded that the arbitration agreement was unconscionable and an appellate court agreed, noting that the rules in the arbitration agreement were "so one-sided that their only possible purpose is to undermine the neutrality of the proceeding."

Among the reasons for this decision: Arbitrators were selected from a list that Hooters created. Hooters could cancel the agreement to arbitrate, but employees could not. Furthermore, Hooters could change the rules of the arbitration at any time.[10]

Key Elements in Your Compliance Program

Even when you are not legally required to adopt a compliance program, it is sound business practice to do so. The Sentencing Guidelines mentioned earlier are the best starting point for developing your program. The Sentencing Commission *Guidelines Manual* states that "to have an effective compliance program" you must "promote an organizational culture that encourages ethical conduct and a commitment to compliance with the law." This means that, at a minimum, your company must meet seven requirements (quoted and summarized from the *Manual*):

1. The organization shall establish standards and procedures to prevent and detect criminal conduct.

2. [Company leaders must] be knowledgeable about the content and operation of the compliance and ethics program and shall exercise reasonable oversight [over its] implementation and

effectiveness. [Company leaders must] ensure that the organization has an effective compliance and ethics program. [They must assign] overall responsibility for the compliance and ethics program. [The standard also discusses day-to-day responsibilities, reporting requirements, supporting resources, authority, and access to company leaders.]

3.   The organization shall use reasonable efforts to [exclude from positions of authority individuals who have] engaged in illegal activities or other conduct inconsistent with an effective compliance and ethics program.

4.   The organization shall take reasonable steps to communicate periodically and in a practical manner its standards and procedures, and other aspects of the compliance and ethics program, to [employees through effective training programs and other forms of communication].

5.   The organization shall take reasonable steps (a) to ensure that the organization's compliance and ethics program is followed, including monitoring and auditing to detect criminal conduct; (b) to evaluate periodically the effectiveness of the organization's compliance and ethics program; and (c) to have and publicize a system, which may include mechanisms that allow for anonymity or confidentiality, whereby the organization's employees and agents may report or seek guidance regarding potential or actual criminal conduct without fear of retaliation.

6.   The organization's compliance and ethics program shall be promoted and enforced consistently throughout the organization through (a) appropriate incentives to perform in accordance with the compliance and ethics program; and (b) appropriate disciplinary measures for engaging in criminal conduct and for failing to take reasonable steps to prevent or detect criminal conduct.

7.   After criminal conduct has been detected, the organization shall take reasonable steps to respond appropriately to [any detected] criminal conduct and to prevent further similar criminal conduct, including making any necessary modifications to the organization's compliance and ethics program.

When you cut through the turgid government prose, several key themes emerge. In plain language, you must:

- **Establish** an effective compliance and ethics program (#1 and #2)
- **Communicate** the program to employees and provide them with training (#4)
- **Monitor and evaluate** the program, including mechanisms for employees to report criminal conduct (#5)
- **Enforce** the program through disciplinary actions (#6)
- **Prevent** criminal conduct from recurring (#7)

In addition to taking their own disciplinary actions, companies who seek favorable treatment at sentencing in the United States must report to the Department of Justice facts about individuals within the company who have violated the law. The reason for this policy, which was adopted in 2015, is that it is often difficult for law enforcement officials to prosecute individuals in large corporations that have many layers of decision making.

Developing Your Code of Conduct

The themes in the Sentencing Guidelines are process oriented; they do not give details about the content of compliance and ethics programs. Companies can provide this content in the form of a code of conduct. Governmental authorities and other institutions worldwide—ranging from the European Commission to Hong Kong's Independent Commission Against Corruption to Brazil's Institute of Corporate Governance—have encouraged companies to develop codes of conduct.[11]

For companies that decide to heed this advice, what should be included in a code? The answer to this question is easy in situations where a code is required. For example, the New York Stock Exchange rule mentioned previously requires that codes of business conduct and ethics include provisions on confidentiality, fair dealing, and compliance with the law, among others.

Sometimes court decisions are important to your determination of what should be included—or excluded—from a company code of conduct. For example, Chapter 3 covered sexual harassment risk management. The chapter emphasized that companies should adopt an anti-harassment policy that includes examples of prohibited acts. But in covering wrongful discharge, Chapter 3 also mentioned the importance of excluding from company policies any language that would imply that employees will be discharged only for cause. In other words, you should include a sexual harassment policy in your code of conduct but exclude any language that might override your employment-at-will policy.

Beyond these examples of required provisions, what should be included in your code of conduct? Professor Paine and her coauthors analyzed several sets of guidelines for multinational companies, the codes of some of the largest companies in the world, and legal requirements for codes. Based on this extensive research, they developed a global consensus based on eight key ethical principles. You can use this consensus list, which they call a "Codex," in developing a code of conduct for your business or in assessing your existing code. The following definitions are quoted from their article "Up to Code."[12]

1. **Fiduciary Principle:** Act as a fiduciary for the company and its investors. Carry out the company's business in a diligent and loyal manner, with the degree of candor expected of a trustee. [As discussed earlier, this principle

is similar to a law-based ethical standard.]

2. **Property Principle:** Respect property and the rights of those who own it. Refrain from theft and misappropriation, avoid waste, and safeguard the property entrusted to you.

3. **Reliability Principle:** Honor commitments. Be faithful to your word and follow through on promises, agreements, and other voluntary undertakings, whether or not embodied in legally enforceable contracts.

4. **Transparency Principle:** Conduct business in a truthful and open manner. Refrain from deceptive acts and practices, keep accurate records, and make timely disclosures of material information while respecting obligations of confidentiality and privacy.

5. **Dignity Principle:** Respect the dignity of all people. Protect the health, safety, privacy, and human rights of others; refrain from coercion; and adopt practices that enhance human development in the workplace, the marketplace, and the community.

6. **Fairness Principle:** Engage in free and fair competition, deal with all parties fairly and equitably and practice nondiscrimination in employment and contracting.

7. **Citizenship Principle:** Act as responsible citizens of the community. Respect the law, protect public goods, cooperate with public authorities, avoid improper involvement in politics and government, and contribute to community betterment.

8. **Responsiveness Principle:** Engage with parties who may have legitimate claims and concerns relating to the company's activities, and be responsive to public needs while recognizing the government's role and jurisdiction

in protecting the public interest.

In their detailed analysis, Paine and her colleagues emphasize that these principles relate to each of the four stakeholders discussed in Chapters 2 through 5—customers, employees, the government (which they called the "public"), and investors—along with competitors and suppliers/partners.

Becoming an Ethical Leader

Developing a compliance program and a code of conduct are necessary to create an ethical company, but not sufficient to do so. An additional element is needed because of what Paine and her colleagues call the "Conduct Gap." This phrase stems from their surveys of employees at companies worldwide, which revealed that there is a gap between what companies should do and what they actually do.[13]

This finding is consistent with the results of the KPMG survey mentioned in Chapter 1. The survey concluded that roughly two-thirds of the respondents had witnessed misconduct in the workplace. As noted in that chapter, one problem with codes of conduct is that companies use a top-down approach when developing the codes. The codes often are framed in terms of general principles that are even broader than religious dictums such as the Ten Commandments.

Here are two suggestions for closing the "Conduct Gap": (1) Use the Three Pillar model to embed the principles from the Codex into everyday ethical decision-making and (2) provide employees with a practical decision-making process and related ethical guidelines.

Use the Three Pillar Model to Embed Ethical Principles into Everyday Decisions

This book has attempted to help you become a legally savvy business leader so that you can better understand the Law Pillar's risk management focus and can close the gap between the Strategy Pillar and the Law Pillar to create value. Closing the gap requires that you understand the interests of key company stakeholders—customers, employees, government, and investors.

When a company understands and acts on stakeholder interests, it often produces guidelines that parallel the eight principles in the Codex. But unlike the Codex principles, which sound as though they were handed down from the mountain top where senior executives reside, these Three Pillar guidelines originate on the front line of business decision making. In other words, using the Three Pillar model enables you to operationalize the more abstract principles in the Codex.

Here are some examples of how Three Pillar guidelines from Chapters 2 through 7 parallel the Codex principles:

- **Chapter 2:** Develop safe products that meet customer needs.
    - o **Codex #5:** Protect the health and safety of others and enhance human development in the marketplace.

- **Chapter 3:** Use honesty and management by fact to attract and retain the best talent.
    - o **Codex #4, #5:** Conduct business in a truthful and honest manner. Enhance human development in the workplace.

- **Chapter 3:** Eliminate all forms of discrimination to enable employees to achieve success.
    - o **Codex #5, #6:** Respect the dignity of all people. Enhance human development in the workplace.

Practice nondiscrimination in employment and contracting.

- **Chapter 4:** Participate in the law-making process. Embrace the law through strong compliance programs. Manage political risks in countries that do not follow the rule of law. Operate on the Regulatory Frontier to identify emerging social issues.
    - ○ **Codex #5, #7, #8:** Enhance human development in the community. Act as responsible citizens of the community. Respect the law, cooperate with public authorities, avoid improper involvement in politics and government, and contribute to the community. Be responsive to public needs while recognizing the government's role and jurisdiction in protecting the public interest.

- **Chapter 5:** Protect your property rights. Consider ways to work cooperatively with other companies by sharing intellectual property.
    - ○ **Codex #2:** Respect property and the rights of those who own it. Safeguard the property entrusted to you.

- **Chapter 6:** Focus on creating contracts that build relationships and create value through commercial affinity instead of legalities.
    - ○ **Codex #3:** Honor commitments. Be faithful to your word and follow through on promises, agreements, and other voluntary undertakings, whether or not embodied in legally enforceable contracts.

- **Chapter 7:** Consider using alternatives to litigation for resolving disputes, such as mediation and arbitration.
    - ○ **Codex #8:** Engage with parties who have legitimate claims.

Use a Practical Decision-Making Process and Related Ethical Guidelines

A second approach to closing the Conduct Gap is to supplement the code of conduct with a practical decision-making process and related ethical guidelines that employees can use in day-to-day decisions. A simple four-step process can suffice for ethical decision making:

1. Define the ethical dilemma and alternatives.
2. Get facts, including the impact on stakeholders.
3. Analyze your alternatives, using generic guidelines.
4. Make your decision.

There are many practical ethical guidelines that you and company employees can use at Step 3.[14] Here are four examples:

First, develop a credo or pledge that clearly states company beliefs. For example, the credo of Johnson & Johnson (J&J) tracks the organization of this book (Chapters 2–5) by first emphasizing the company's responsibilities to consumers of its products and then, in descending order, its responsibilities to employees, the community, and stockholders. Here are the opening lines of the J&J credo: "We believe our first responsibility is to the doctors, nurses and patients, to mothers and fathers and all others who use our products and services." Former company CEO Robert Wood Johnson wrote the credo in 1943 and it has guided the company ever since.

Second, when confronted with an ethical concern, think of someone you admire and ask yourself what that person would do to resolve the dilemma. This could be, for example, someone you read about—perhaps an historical figure—or someone you observe at work.

An attorney for Qualcomm once explained why he admired Qualcomm CEO Irwin Jacobs. During negotiations the attorney was involved in, the other side accidentally sent him a fax that appeared to provide confidential information about the negotiations. As he tells the story, "I ran into Irwin's office with the fax. But before I could even start to read it, he asked, 'Was it meant to go to us?' When I told him it wasn't, he said, 'Send it back.' I left with my tail between my legs. He's a very ethical person. Most people would have read that document."[15]

Third, think about how you would feel telling your family about your business decisions. Or how you would feel reading about your actions on the front page of the local newspaper? Sometimes these "family" and "newspaper" tests are combined. As legendary investor Warren Buffett put it: "After they first obey all rules, I then want employees to ask themselves whether they are willing to have any contemplated act appear the next day on the front page of their local paper, to be read by their spouses, children, and friends."

Fourth, consider using the Golden Rule, which is part of every major religion in the world. Although the precise wording differs, the rule basically suggests that you should treat others as you want to be treated.

Your challenge as an ethical leader doesn't stop here. After encouraging employees in your business to use the simple process and guidelines for making day-to-day decisions, you must also "walk the talk." Here's an example. In 1982, beginning with the death of a twelve-year-old girl, seven people in the Chicago area died suddenly over a three-day period. Someone had obtained bottles of Tylenol, added cyanide, and returned the bottles to various stores. The crime was never solved and is still under investigation.

Before the murders, the manufacturer of Tylenol, J&J, held 35% market share. After the murders, the market share plunged to 7%. The ethical dilemma (Step One of the decision-making process) J&J faced was clear: the company had to decide what action to take for a problem it did not cause. At Step Two, the company worked closely with the Chicago Police and the FBI in reviewing facts and developing possible courses of action, including a product recall.

In analyzing the alternatives (Step Three), J&J leaders realized that a recall would have a huge financial impact, as it would involve pulling thirty-one million bottles of Tylenol (with a value of $100 million) from shelves nationwide. But they also had the benefit of the clear credo described earlier. In the words of company CEO James Burke, "The credo made it very clear at that point exactly what we were all about. It gave me the ammunition I needed to persuade shareholders and others to spend the $100 million on the recall. The credo helped sell it."[16]

With this credo to guide the company's leaders, their decision (Step Four) to recall the product became clear. The company then quickly developed tamper-proof packaging, reintroduced the product, and eventually regained its market share leadership.

In addition to resolving specific ethical dilemmas in a beneficial manner, when company leaders like Burke establish a culture of integrity by "walking the talk," they have an opportunity to create value for their companies. A recent study of employees concluded that "when employees perceived high levels of integrity at work, their companies were more productive, more attractive to potential new hires, and more profitable."[17]

Beyond Business Decision-Making: Corporate Social Responsibility

This chapter has emphasized the elements that encourage company leaders and employees to make ethical decisions in their daily work: use law-based and ethical standards, develop a compliance program and a code of conduct, and use a simple decision-making process that includes practical ethical guidelines. But what about large-scale strategic decisions that change the direction of the company? Can and should business leaders decide to use company resources to serve society in addition to creating value for shareholders?

These questions bring us full circle back to Chapter 1, which concluded that the law does not require company leaders to maximize shareholder value. Indeed, most state laws authorize them to consider the interests of all stakeholders, including the community at large. Furthermore, some laws now even require companies to engage in some form of corporate social responsibility ("CSR"), ranging from regulations covering conflict minerals to the European Union requiring companies to report on sustainability. According to two legal experts, "we are now witnessing a transition from voluntary CSR measures to hard law by means of... law and regulations in the United States and around the globe."[18]

Regardless of whether CSR strategies are voluntary or required by law, many business leaders undoubtedly would like to develop strategies that benefit both shareholders and society. This involves moving beyond the fixed-pie assumption that was discussed in Chapter 1 and reframing strategies in order to consider the interests of both the company and society. When this happens, companies can achieve the desired overlap among the Three Pillars and create a zone of sustainable competitive advantage.

A strategy that has the goal of benefitting society while also creating shareholder value obviously brings into play the Strategy Pillar and the Ethics Pillar. But what is the role of the Law Pillar? This question was addressed implicitly by Harvard strategy professor Michael Porter and his coauthor Mark Kramer in their article "Strategy and Society." The ideas in their article are closely aligned with those in this chapter in that they proposed "a new way to look at the relationship between business and society that does not treat corporate success and social welfare as a zero-sum game."[19]

According to the authors, this "new look" arises from an analysis based on the two forms of interdependence between companies and society: inside-out links and outside-in links. Inside-out links focus on the ways in which companies affect society through their normal business operations, whereas outside-in links deal with how social conditions impact companies. An understanding of these links enables companies to "set an affirmative CSR agenda that produces maximum social benefit as well as gains for the business."[20]

The authors draw on Porter's earlier work to suggest the type of analysis that enables companies to prioritize the social issues they want to address. For analyzing inside-out links, the authors recommend a value chain analysis that produces a large array of social issues that are replete with legal ramifications. These include discrimination, government regulations, lobbying, privacy, safe working conditions, truthful advertising, and worker safety.

For the outside-in analysis, the authors recommend a diamond framework with four elements: (1) the context for firm strategy, (2) local demand conditions, (3) related and supporting industries, and (4) input conditions. As one might expect, the law plays a large role in this analysis. The authors list these examples of the first element, the context for firm strategy:

- Fair and open local competition (e.g., fair regulations)
- Intellectual property protection
- Transparency (e.g., corruption)
- Rule of law (e.g., protection of property)
- Meritocratic incentive systems (e.g., antidiscrimination)

So achieving the twin goals of business success and social responsibility, like the other business goals discussed throughout this book, requires considering all three pillars of decision making— Strategy, Law, and Ethics. Exploring stakeholder interests through the lens of the Three Pillar model enables companies to benefit others while also benefitting themselves. In this way, companies have an opportunity to embody at a company level the advice on happiness that economist John Stuart Mill gave to individuals: "Those only are happy... who have their minds fixed on some object other than their own happiness; on the happiness of others, on the improvement of mankind.... Aiming thus at something else, they find happiness by the way."[21]

Notes

Chapter 1

1. Savage, "How 4 Federal Lawyers Paved the Way to Kill Osama bin Laden," *The New York Times*, October 28, 2015
2. *Id.*
3. *Journal of Business Ethics*, September 1997
4. "Corporate Social Responsibility: A Three-Domain Approach," *Business Ethics Quarterly*, October 2003
5. "An Education in Ethics," *Harvard Magazine*, September–October 2006
6. Datar, Garvin, and Cullen, *Rethinking the MBA* (2010)
7. Leadership and Corporate Accountability, Course Syllabus, http://www.hbs.edu/rethinking-the-mba/docs/harvard-business-school-leadership-and-corporate-accountability-2011-course-syllabus.pdf
8. "The Basic LCA Framework," Harvard Business School N9-315-060
9. "Instructor's Guide to Leadership and Corporate Accountability," Harvard Business School 5-307-032
10. *Harvard Business Review*, February 2003
11. "Who Let the Lawyers Out?: Reconstructing the Role of the Chief Legal Officer and the Corporate Client in a Globalizing World," *University of Pennsylvania Journal of Business Law*, forthcoming
12. Pierson, *The Education of American Businessmen* (1959)
13. Leinwand and Mainardi, "Rethinking the Function of Business Functions," February 2013

14. *Strategy and Structure* (1962)
15. *Competitive Advantage* (1985)
16. "Managing Your Lawyers," January–February 1983
17. "Coase Was Clear: Laws Can Cure or Kill," October 21, 1991
18. *International Law for Business* (1994)
19. "Making International Law an Integral Part of the International Business Program," *The Journal of Legal Studies Education*, December 1994
20. "2014 US Business Needs for Employees with International Expertise," http://www.wm.edu/offices/revescenter/internation alization/papers%20and%20presentations/danielkediafull.pdf
21. Siedel, "Six Forces and the Legal Environment of Business," *American Business Law Journal*, Summer 2000
22. March–April 1990
23. Harrison, "Champions of Change," *InsideCounsel*, November 1, 2014
24. *AMBA Executive*, September 1997
25. "Volkswagen Diesel Scandal," *Chicago Tribune*, September 22, 2015
26. Masters, "Bankers Not Only Ones Pushing Ethical Boundaries," September 25, 2015
27. "Lessons Learned in Business School," August 20, 2002
28. Gilbert and Kent, "BP Agrees to Pay $18.7 Billion to Settle Deepwater Horizon Oil Spill Claims," *Wall Street Journal*, July 2, 2015
29. Bagley et al., *supra*
30. Director's Roundtable, "Michael Solender," September 29, 2015
31. "List of Areas of Law," http://en. wikipedia.org/wiki/List_ of_areas_of_law
32. Refo, "The Vanishing Trial," *Litigation*, Winter 2004
33. "The Status of Law in Academic Business Study," http://cba2 .unomaha.edu/faculty/mohara/web/ALSBsta8.htm
34. "Value Creation by Lawyers," *The Yale Law Journal*, December 1984

35. "What is Strategy?," November–December 1996
36. "Value Creation by Lawyers," *supra*
37. Harrison, "Champions of Change," *InsideCounsel*, November 1, 2014
38. *Skills for the 21st Century General Counsel* (2013)
39. "The American Business Law Journal at Fifty," *ABLJ*, Spring 2013
40. "2015 Travelers Business Risk Index," http://www.travelers .com/prepare-prevent/risk-index/business/2015/business-risk-index-report.pdf
41. "Risk Management for an Era of Greater Uncertainty," http:// www.accenture.com/us-en/~/media/Accenture/Conversion-Assets/DotCom/Documents/Global/PDF/Industries_6/Accent ure-Global-Risk-Management-Study-2013.pdf
42. "2015 Litigation Trends Annual Survey," http://www.norton rosefulbright.com/files/20150514-2015-litigation-trends-survey_v24-128746.pdf
43. AlixPartners Litigation and Corporate Compliance Survey, http://www.alixpartners.com/en/LinkClick.aspx?fileticket=S O5aBoKEHDs%3d&tabid=635
44. "Legal Risk Benchmarking Survey," http://www.blplaw.com /download/BLP_Legal_Risk_Benchmarking_Report.pdf
45. "Managing Complexity and Change in a New Landscape," http://www.ey.com/Publication/vwLUAssets/EY_-_7_big_ changes_to_asset_management_operating_models/$FILE/ EY-Managing-complexity-and-change-in-a-new-landscape. pdf
46. "Government and the Global CEO: Redefining Success in a Changing World," http://www.pwc.com/gx/en/industries/ government-public-services/public-sector-research-centre/ publications/government-19th-annual-ceo-survey.html
47. "Rediscovering the Power of Law in Business Education," http://www.aacsb.edu/blog/2016/february/rediscovering-the-power-of-law-in-business-education
48. "Building the Manager's Toolbox, *Journal of Legal Studies*

Education, 2013

49. *Skills for the 21st Century General Counsel, supra*
50. *Id.*
51. Siedel, *Negotiating for Success: Essential Strategies and Skills* (2014)
52. Jessen, "Moving Beyond the 'Department of No,'" *Inside Counsel,* December 11, 2015
53. Legal Risk Benchmarking Survey," *supra*
54. Khusainova, "Exploring Legal Strategy," unpublished paper
55. "Law, Strategy and Competitive Advantage," *Connecticut Law Review,* November 2011
56. "Finding the Right Corporate Legal Strategy," Fall 2014
57. "Legal Risk Benchmarking Survey," *supra*
58. "Building Your Organizations Legal IQ," http://img.en25 .com/Web/CEB/CEB_Legal_Building_Your_Organizations_ Legal_IQ_Preview_Report.pdf?cid=70134000001A7ckAAC
59. "The 190/MBA Program, The University of Chicago Booth School of Business, undated catalog
60. Bagley, et al., *supra*
61. Colby, Ehrlich, Sullivan and Dolle, *Rethinking Undergraduate Business Education* (2011)
62. "A Seat at the Table," http://www.shell.com/global/about shell/media/speeches-and-articles/2014/a-seat-at-the-table-in-house-lawyers-are-business-partners.html
63. Bagley, et al., *supra*
64. Russo and Schoemaker, *Decision Traps* (1990)
65. *Judgment in Managerial Decision Making* (2008)
66. Siedel, *Negotiating for Success, supra*
67. "Managing Government Relations for the Future," http:// www.mckinsey.com/insights/public_sector/managing_govern ment_relations_for_the_future_mckinsey_global_survey_resu lts
68. Nordic School of Proactive Law, http://www.proactivelaw .org/
69. Berger-Walliser and Ostergaard, eds., 2012

70. *Harvard Business Review*, January–February 2011
71. Lewis, *The Public Image of Henry Ford* (1976)
72. "Why We Should Stop Teaching *Dodge v. Ford*," http://papers.ssrn.com/sol3/papers.cfm?abstract_id=1013744
73. KPMG, "Integrity Survey," http://www.kpmg.com/CN/en/IssuesAndInsights/ArticlesPublications/Documents/Integrity-Survey-2013-O-201307.pdf
74. Gibeaut, "Getting Your House in Order," *ABAJ*, June 1999
75. Gellman, "M.B.A.s Get Lessons in Income Inequality," *Wall Street Journal*, November 4, 2015

Chapter 2

1. Wysocki, "Manufacturers Are Hit with More Lawsuits," *Wall Street Journal*, June 3, 1976
2. Zeman and Fix, "When Secrecy Explodes," *Detroit Free Press*, July 7, 2000
3. Geisel, "Gun Firm Pays $6.8 Million to Attorney," *Business Insurance*, November 13, 1978
4. McGuire, *The Impact of Product Liability* (1988)
5. *Banks v. ICI* (1994)
6. *Prosser and Keeton on the Law of Torts* (1984)
7. Edgerton, "How One Firm Learned Its Lesson in Liability Cases," *Detroit Free Press*, March 19, 1978
8. Perlman, "Riddell Severed From NFL Claims in Concussion MDL," *Law 360*, December 1, 2015
9. *Cipollone v. Liggett Group, Inc.* (1990)
10. Belson, "Warning Labels on Helmets Combat Injury and Liability," *The New York Times*, August 4, 2013
11. *Bravman v. Baxter Healthcare Corporation* (1993)
12. Geyelin, "Yes, $145 Billion Deals Tobacco a Huge Blow, But Not a Killing One," July 17, 2000
13. Greene, "Peeking Beneath the Corporate Veil," August 13, 1984

14. *Uniroyal v. Martinez* (1998)
15. Barksdale (ed.), *Marketing in Progress* (1964)

Chapter 3

1. Chubb, *Worth the Risk* (2013)
2. Cranman and Baum, "Approach to Your Employment Law Audit," *ACC Docket*, March 2007
3. *Toussaint v. Blue Cross & Blue Shield* (1980)
4. *Fortune v. National Cash Register Company* (1977)
5. *Wagenseller v. Scottsdale Memorial Hospital* (1985)
6. *Hill v. Buck* (1984)
7. "Performance Evaluations Worst Practices," http://manpower groupblogs.us/employment_blawg/2012/01/12/performance-evaluations-worst-practices/
8. Reuss, "$61 Million Awarded for Firing," *Times Tribune*, April 5, 1985
9. Sella, "More Big Bucks in Jury Verdicts," *ABAJ*, July 1989
10. Varchaver, "Turmoil at Triton," *American Lawyer*, March 1993
11. Chassany, "Decay of the Permanent Job as France Balks at Labour Reform," *Financial Times*, August 11, 2015
12. Adler and Peirce, "The Legal, Ethical, and Social Implications of the 'Reasonable Woman' Standard," *Fordham Law Review*, 1993
13. Susman Godfrey, "Libel/Slander Litigation," http://www.susmangodfrey.com/practice/libel.html
14. *Zechman v. Merrill Lynch* (1990)
15. *Lewis v. Equitable* (1986)
16. Dertouzos and Karoly, *Labor Market Responses to Employer Liability* (1992)
17. DuFresnes, "Honest Employee Evaluations, *World Reports*, July–September 1994
18. Schoenberger, "The Risk of Reviews," *Wall Street Journal*,

October 26, 2015

19. "Trust in Me," *The Economist*, December 16, 1995

20. Fuchs, "The 8 Largest Sexual Harassment Verdicts in History," *Business Insider*, September 3, 2012

21. Sullivan, "Sexual Harassment Matters," *In House*, December 21, 2015

22. "Harassment," EEOC, http://www.eeoc.gov/laws/types/ harassment .cfm

23. Orrick, Herrington, and Sutcliffe, "New Definition of Sexual Harassment," http://www.lexology.com/library/detail.aspx ?g=df743079-0af7-4eea-8f70-65b66826edd9

24. "Nasty, but Rarer," November 12, 2011

25. *Faragher v. City of Boca Raton* (1998)

26. Machlowitz and Machlowitz, "Preventing Sexual Harassment," *ABAJ*, October 1, 1987

27. *Robinson v. Jacksonville Shipyards* (1991)

28. *Fenton v. Hisan* (1999)

29. *Thompson v. North American Stainless* (2011)

30. "Retaliation—Making It Personal," http://www.eeoc.gov /laws/types/retaliation_considerations.cfm

31. Aronson, "Justices' Sex Harassment Decisions Spark Fears," *National Law Journal*, November 9, 1998

32. Segal, "Getting Serious About Sexual Harassment," *Business Week*, November 2, 1992

33. Gallucci, "90 Percent of Female Restaurant Workers Sexually Harassed," *Observer*, October 8, 2014

34. "Stop Violence Against Women," http://www.stopvaw.org/ sexual_harassment

35. Albo, "The Percentages of Women Who Have Been Sexually Harassed in Public Are Staggering," *Good*, January 20, 2016

36. "Sexual Harassment," http://www.eeoc.gov/eeoc/statistics/ enforcement/sexual_harassment.cfm

37. Barrier, "Sexual Harassment," *Nation's Business*, December, 1998

38. McMorris, "Employees Face Greater Liability in Race Cases,"

Wall Street Journal, July 1, 1999

39. *Booker v. Budget Rent-A-Car Systems* (1998)
40. *Lockard v. Pizza Hut* (1998)
41. *Pryor v. United Air Lines* (2015)
42. "Dow Recognized for Support of Lesbian, Gay, Bisexual and Transgender Rights," http://www.dow.com/en-US/ne ws/press-releases/Dow%20Recognized%20for%20Suppor t%20of%20Lesbian%20Gay%20Bisexual%20and%20Tran sgender%20Rights#q=respect%20and%20responsibility&t =All
43. Lublin, "New Report Finds a Diversity Dividend at Work," *Wall Street Journal,* January 20, 2015

Chapter 4

1. Musters, Parekh and Ramkumar, "Organizing the Government-Affairs Function for Impact," *McKinsey Quarterly,* November 2013
2. "Beyond Corporate Social Responsibility," http://www. mckinsey.com/insights/strategy/beyond_corporate_social_res ponsibility_integrated_external_engagement
3. Wallison, "Four Years of Dodd-Frank Damage," *Wall Street Journal,* July 20, 2014
4. "The Rise of the Fourth Branch of Government," *The Washington Post,* May 24, 2013
5. "Twitter Settles Charges That It Failed to Protect Consumers' Personal Information," http://www.ftc.gov/news-events/press-releases/2010/06/twitter-settles-charges-it-failed-protect-consumers-personal
6. "The Rise of the Fourth Branch of Government," *supra*
7. JPMorgan Chase & Co., http://careers.jpmorganchase.com /career/jpmc/careers/lob
8. Calmes and Story, "In Washington, One Bank Chief Still Holds Sway," *The New York Times,* July 18, 2009

9. "Political Activities," http://www.gesustainability.com/enab ling-progress/political-activities/

10. *Academy of Management Review*, October 1986

11. "Kentucky Senate Race," http://www.opensecrets.org/races/ summary.php?id=KYS1&cycle=2014

12. "What is a PAC?" http://www.opensecrets.org/pacs/pacfaq .php

13. This data is from OpenSecrets.org, http://www.opensecrets .org/

14. "Advocacy Advertising," http://www.allbusiness.com/barr ons_dictionary/dictionary-advocacy-advertising-4950473- 1.html

15. "OpenSecrets.org," http://www.opensecrets.org/

16. *Id.*

17. Hamburger and Gold, "Google, Once Disdainful of Lobbying, Now a Master of Washington Influence," April 12, 2014

18. Marchi and Parekh, "How the Sharing Economy Can Make Its Case," *McKinsey Quarterly*, December 2015

19. Grimaldi, *Bow Tie Banker* (2008)

20. Newman, "Why Mark Zuckerberg is Getting Political," *US News & World Report*, March 27, 2013

21. Adapted from Siedel, *Using the Law for Competitive Advantage* (2002)

22. McGrane and Steinberg, "Wall Street Adapts to New Regulatory Regime," *Wall Street Journal*, July 21, 2014

23. "Rediscovering the Power of Law in Business Education," http://www.aacsb.edu/blog/2016/february/rediscovering-the- power-of-law-in-business-education

24. Culp, Werthen, Frei and Schelling, "Turning Regulatory Challenges into Business Opportunities," December 2014

25. Adapted from Siedel, *supra*

26. *Id.*

27. *Sottera v. FDA* (2010)

28. Whitney, "Apple, Samsung to Return to Court in 2016 for Next Round of Patent War," *CNET*, September 2, 2015.

29. Smith and Eder, "How Apple Got Its Case Across," *Wall Street Journal*, August 26, 2012

30. "How to Mitigate Political Risk," *Stanford Business*, Autumn 2015

31. Bonini, Mendonca and Oppenheim, "When Social Issues Become Strategic," March 2006

32. Bagley, et al., "Who Let the Lawyers Out?" *University of Pennsylvania Law Journal of Business Law*, forthcoming

33. Bonini and Swartz, "Bringing Discipline to Your Sustainability Initiatives," August 2014

34. Porter and Kramer, "Creating Shared Value," *Harvard Business Review*, January–February 2011

35. "Southwest Airlines," http://en.wikipedia.org/wiki/Southwest _Airlines#Early_history

36. Marchi and Parekh, *supra*

37. "Creative Destruction Legal Conflict: Lawyers as Disruption Framers in Entrepreneurship," http://papers.ssrn.com/sol3/papers.cfm?abstract_id=2692833

38. Chen, "At $68 Billion Valuation, Uber Will Be Bigger Than GM, Ford, and Honda," *Forbes*, December 4, 2015

39. Macmillan and Fleisher, "How Sharp-Elbowed Uber Is Trying to Make Nice," *Wall Street Journal*, January 29, 2015

Chapter 5

1. World Intellectual Property Organization (WIPO) website, http://www.wipo.int/portal/en/index.html

2. Mai-Duc, "All the 'Happy Birthday' Song Copyright Claims Are Invalid, Federal Judge Rules," *Los Angeles Times*, September 22, 2015

3. WIPO Website, http://www.wipo.int/about-ip/en/

4. History of Rice Cultivation at Ricepedia, http://ricepedia.org /culture/history-of-rice-cultivation

5. Encyclopaedia Britannica, "Charles Babbage, British Inventor

and Mathematician," http://www.britannica.com/biography/
Charles-Babbage

6. Sailo, "Decoding the Value of Intellectual Property," *iRunway*, January 28, 2015
7. Lin, "Executive Trade Secrets," *Notre Dame Law Review*, 2012
8. McManus, "10 Trade Secrets We Wish We Knew," *Money: How Stuff Works*, http://money.howstuffworks.com/10-tradesecrets.htm
9. Library of Congress Website, http://www.loc.gov/law/help/tradesecrets/
10. *Id.*
11. *Id.*
12. WIPO Website, http://www.wipo.int/patents/en/
13. WIPO Magazine, "Bioethics and Patent Law: The Case of the Oncomouse," June 2006
14. "Pharmaceutical Composition Containing, Cow Urine Distillate and an Antibiotic," http://www.google.com/patents/US6410059
15. *Association for Molecular Pathology v. Myriad Genetics* (2013)
16. Shear and Kelley, "A Researcher's Guide to Patents," *Plant Physiology*, July 2003
17. WIPO Website, http://www.wipo.int/patents/en/faq_patents.html
18. PatentaDesign.com Website, http://www.thoughtstopaper.com/patentadesign.com/knowledge/understanding-design-patents.html
19. Swanson, "The Growing Allure of Plant Patenting for Brand Differentiation," *Earth and Table Law Reporter*, July 9, 2012
20. World Trade Organization (WTO) Website, TRIPS Agreement, http://www.wto.org/english/tratop_e/trips_e/t_agm0_e.htm
21. The Thomas Edison Papers, Rutgers University, Patent Interference Files–Sawyer and Man v. Edison
22. "Improvement in Combined Knives, Forks, and Spoons," http://www.google.com/patents/US147119?dq=147119&hl=en&sa=X&ved=0ahUKEwju1M3zkLTKAhUBEGMKHUSRBy4Q6AEIHTAA

23. WIPO Website, http://www.wipo.int/patents/en/faq_patents .html
24. USPTO Website, http://www.uspto.gov/trademarks-getting-started/trademark-basics/trademark-patent-or-copyright
25. Goldman, "Google Successfully Defends Its Most Valuable Asset in Court," *Forbes*, September 15, 2014
26. International Trademark Association, Trademark Basics, http://www.inta.org/Media/Documents/2012_TMBasicsBusiness.pdf
27. *Id.*
28. United States Patent and Trademark Office (USPTO), http://www.uspto.gov/trademark/soundmarks/trademark-sound-mark-examples
29. O'Dell, "Harley-Davidson Quits Trying to Hog Sound," *Los Angeles Times*, June 21, 2000
30. "Swoosh," http://en.wikipedia.org/wiki/Swoosh
31. ConceptDrop, "How Nike Redefined the Power of Brand Image," October 23, 2013
32. Brettman, "Nike Hits $30 Billion in Revenue For Fiscal Year 2015," *The Oregonian*, June 25, 2015
33. International Trademark Association, Trademark Basics, http://www.inta.org/Media/Documents/2012_TMBasicsBusiness.pdf
34. Novack, "Google Was Originally Called BackRub," *Gizmodo*, July 15, 2014
35. International Trademark Association, Trademark Basics, http://www.inta.org/Media/Documents/2012_TMBasicsBusiness.pdf
36. "*Apple Corps v. Apple Computer*," http://en.wikipedia.org/wiki/Apple_Corps_v_Apple_Computer
37. International Trademark Association, Trademark Basics, http://www.inta.org/Media/Documents/2012_TMBasicsBusiness.pdf
38. *Two Pesos, Inc. v. Taco Cabana, Inc.* (1992)
39. "*Two Pesos, Inc. v. Taco Cabana, Inc.*," http://en.wikipedia

.org/wiki/Two_Pesos,_Inc._v._Taco_Cabana,_Inc.

40. Miller, *Where There's Life, There's Lawsuits* (2003)
41. "A Moron in a Hurry," http://en.wikipedia.org/wiki/A_moron _in_a_hurry
42. "Trademark," http://en.wikipedia.org/wiki/Trademark
43. International Trademark Association, Trademark Basics, http: //www.inta.org/Media/Documents/2012_TMBasicsBusiness.p df
44. US Copyright Office, "Copyright Basics," May 2012
45. "List of Countries' Copyright Lengths," http://en.wikipedia .org/wiki/List_of_countries%27_copyright_lengths"
46. *Rupa Marya, et al. v. Warner/Chappell Music, Inc., et al.* (2015)
47. "Napster," http://en.wikipedia.org/wiki/Napster
48. Kumar, "Well-Known Cases of Copyright Infringement," *Bright Hub*, March 17, 2011
49. *Swatch Group v. Bloomberg* (2014)
50. Tenuto, "Warner Bros. Settles Tyson Tattoo Case over Hangover II," *Article3*, June 21, 2011
51. "Fair Dealing," http://en.wikipedia.org/wiki/Fair_dealing
52. *"Oracle Corp. v. SAP AG,"* http://en.wikipedia.org/wiki/Ora cle_Corp._v._SAP_AG
53. Kestenbaum, "One Man's Mission to Bring Back Hydrox Cookies," *NPR News Report*, September 24, 2015
54. "PageRank," http://en.wikipedia.org/wiki/PageRank
55. Lincoln, "Lecture on Discoveries and Inventions," April 6, 1858, Abraham Lincoln Online, http://www.abrahamlincoln online.org/lincoln/speeches/discoveries.htm
56. Arndt, "IBM's Crafty Intellectual Property Strategy," *Business Week*, December 8, 2008
57. "Smartphone Patent Wars," http://en.wikipedia.org/wiki/Sma rtphone_patent_wars
58. Scott, "The Radio Inventor/Entrepreneurs," http://www.west ga.edu/~bquest/2001/radio.htm
59. "Gemstar-TV Guide International," http://en.wikipedia.org/ wiki/Gemstar-TV_Guide_International

60. Gollin, *Driving Innovation: Intellectual Property Strategies for a Dynamic World* (2008)
61. "Shop Names," http://shop.com.co.domains.blog.ir/1391/10/02/.COM
62. O'Reilly, "Piracy is Progressive Taxation, and Other Thoughts on the Evolution of Online Distribution," openp2p.com, December 11, 2002
63. Schlackman, "Do Night Photos of the Eiffel Tower Violate Copyright?" *Art Law Journal*, November 16, 2014
64. Gollin, *supra*
65. "How Google Makes Improvements to Its Search Algorithm," http://www.youtube.com/watch?v=J5RZOU6vK4Q
66. *Id.*
67. Alter, "God vs. Gridiron," *Wall Street Journal*, February 2, 2008
68. Gray, "A New Era in IP Licensing," *The Licensing Journal*, Volume 28 No.10, November/December 2008
69. WIPO Website, "The Coffee War," http://www.wipo.int/ipadvantage/en/details.jsp?id=2621
70. "Patent Pool," http://en.wikipedia.org/wiki/Patent_pool
71. Munger, "A Dozen Things I've Learned about Business from Bill Gates," *25iq*, July 2014

Chapter 6

1. Miller, *Fundamentals of Business Law* (2012)
2. Curriden, "Joe Jamail,"*ABA Journal*, March 2, 2009
3. *Lucy v. Zehmer* (1954)
4. http://www2.iaccm.com/resources/?id=7619
5. Stein and Harris, "Bulletproof," http://www.hcc.com/DivisionsProducts/HCCSpecialty/Products/ProfessionalLiability/ArchitectsEngineersContractorsProfLiability/RiskManagementLibrary/RiskManagementLibrary/BulletproofLimitationofLiabilityinDesignPro/tabid/442/Default.aspx

6. University of Texas System, "Indemnification Sample Clauses"
7. *PLC Law Department Quarterly*, October–December, 2005
8. See note 4, *supra*
9. "Best practices in commercial contracting," in *A Proactive Approach* (2006)
10. Adapted from Ruuki, *Framework Agreement for Purchasing Services*

Chapter 7

1. "Attorneys' Use of ADR is Crucial to Their Willingness to Recommend It to Clients," *Dispute Resolution Magazine*, Winter 2000
2. "Lions of the Trial Bar," *ABA Journal*, March 2009
3. Gandhi, *An Autobiography: The Story of My Experiments With Truth* (1927)
4. *Wake Forest Law Review*, 2014, quoted in Lande, "Litigation as Violence," *Mediate.com*
5. Jacobs, "'Were You Alone or by Yourself?' And Other Courtroom Gaffes," *Wall Street Journal*, June 15, 1998
6. "Now Try Collecting," *The Economist*, August 2, 2014
7. AAA (2008)
8. *Palo Alto v. Service Employees International Union* (1999)
9. AAA, *Optional Appellate Arbitration Rules*
10. Zuckerman, "Comparing Costs in Construction Arbitration & Litigation," *Dispute Resolution Journal*, May/July 2007
11. "Companies Adopting Postal Service Grievance Process," *The New York Times*, September 6, 2000
12. *Avista Management v. Wausau Underwriters* (2006)
13. For further information, see http://www.npr.org/templates/story/story.php?storyId=4812658
14. "Corporate Pledge," http://www.cpradr.org/PracticeAreas/ADRPledges/CorporatePledgeSigners.aspx
15. "Sample Business Contracts," http://contracts.onecle.com/

16. CPR, *Corporate Dispute Management* (1982)
17. Seigel, "Jury Awards Connie Francis 42.5 Million in Westbury Rape," *The New York Times*, July 2, 1976
18. AAA (2009)
19. Block, "UMHS Malpractice Approach Wins Praise," *The Michigan Daily*, January 10, 2013
20. "Why Mediation is Important," http://www.pon.harvard.edu /daily/mediation/mediation-in-transactional-negotiation-2/
21. O'Connell, "Company Lawyers Sniff Out Revenue," May 13, 2011
22. *Notre Dame Law Review*, 2015
23. "Rediscovering the Power of Law in Business Education," http://www.aacsb.edu/blog/2016/february/rediscovering- the-power-of-law-in-business-education

Chapter 8

1. "Legal Compliance Programs," Harvard Business School 9-306-014 (2005)
2. The examples in this section are drawn from "Corporate Compliance Survey," *The Business Lawyer*, August 2005
3. *In re Caremark International, Inc. Derivative Litigation*
4. "Legal Compliance Programs," *supra*
5. Paine, "Managing for Organizational Integrity," *Harvard Business Review*, March–April 1994
6. This section is adapted from Siedel, *Negotiating for Success: Essential Strategies and Skills* (2014)
7. Schrotenboer, "Lance Armstrong Wins Endorsement Lawsuit," *USA Today*, February 26, 2014
8. *Ikeda v. Curtis* (1953)
9. *Spratlin v. Hawn* (1967)
10. *Hooters v. Phillips* (1998)
11. Paine, Deshpande, Margolis and Bettcher, "Up to Code," *Harvard Business Review*, December 2005

12. *Id.*
13. Paine, Deshpande and Margolis, "A Global Leader's Guide to Managing Business Conduct," *Harvard Business Review*, September 2011
14. Adapted from Siedel, *supra*
15. Foster, "Qualcomm Counsel Hits the Jackpot," *National Law Journal*, January 31, 2000
16. "Tylenol and the Legacy of J&J's James Burke," http://knowledge.wharton.upenn.edu/article/tylenol-and-the-legacy-of-jjs-james-burke/. Another source used in summarizing the Tylenol case is "Chicago Tylenol Murders," http://en.wikipedia.org/wiki/Chicago_Tylenol_murders
17. "Corporate Culture Gets Real," *BizEd*, September–October 2015
18. Walter and Shackelford, "Our Mini-Theme: Corporate Social Responsibility Is Now Legal," *Business Law Today*, http://www.americanbar.org/publications/blt/2015/01/intro.html
19. *Harvard Business Review*, December 2006
20. *Id.*
21. *Autobiography of John Stuart Mill* (1873)

CPSIA information can be obtained
at www.ICGtesting.com
Printed in the USA
FSHW011315150120
66124FS

9 780997 056600